THE GARDENER'S GUIDE TO PLANT DISEASES

EARTH-SAFE REMEDIES

Barbara Pleasant

Storey Publishing

ACKNOWLEDGMENTS

Grateful acknowledgment to the many plant pathologists whose work has made this book possible, with special thanks to Dr. Phil Dukes for his patient and valuable assistanse.

The mission of Storey Publishing is to serve our customers by publishing practical information that encourages personal independence in harmony with the environment.

Edited by Deborah Balmuth and Elizabeth P. Stell
Cover design by Meredith Maker
Text design by Michelle Arabia, Andrea Gray, and Greg Imhoff
Text production by Andrea Gray
Line drawings by Mary Thompson
Indexed by Northwind Editorial Services

The information in this book is true and complete to the best of our knowledge. All recommendations are made without guarantee on the part of the author or Storey Publishing. The author and publisher disclaim any liability in connection with the use of this information. For additional information, please contact Storey Publishing, 210 MASS MOCA Way, North Adams, MA 01247.

Storey books are available for special premium and promotional uses and for customized editions. For further information, please call 1-800-793-9396.

Printed in the United States by Versa Press
10 9 8 7

Library of Congress Cataloging-in-Publication Data

Pleasant, Barbara.
      The gardener's guide to plant diseases : earth-safe remedies / Barbara Pleasant.
            p.   cm.
      Includes index.
      ISBN 978-0-88266-274-9 (pbk.)
      1. Garden pests — Biological control. 2. Plant diseases. 3. Plants,
            Protection of. 4. Organic gardening. I. Title.
SB974.P58   1995
635'.049'097—dc20   94-34067
                                                                                              CIP

TABLE OF CONTENTS

Introduction

The purpose of this book is to provide gardeners with information on the common diseases that affect garden plants. You don't need a special vocabulary to manage garden diseases, or to read this book. In writing each entry, my primary mission has been to translate scientific information and data into ideas that can be easily understood by any reader who is faced with disease problems and seeks to know what to do about them.

The scientific names of the organisms that cause common plant diseases are included for students who might use this book as a starting place for further scientific inquiry. Yet for most gardeners, it is much more important to understand the process at work when a disease outbreak occurs than the name or family affiliation of the fungus, bacteria, nematode, or virus responsible for the problem.

As a longtime organic gardener living in a warm, humid climate where some disease is usually present in the garden, I have long been frustrated with the dearth of usable guidance for earth-safe disease control provided by many otherwise excellent garden reference books. Since we gardeners work on a very small scale compared to fruit and vegetable farmers, many standard remedies — like reapplying fungicides every time it rains — simply do not fit our needs.

Throughout this book, I have sought to provide workable solutions for gardeners who keep home-sized vegetable plots along with a small, select collection of fruits. In situations where a farmer might spray fungicides once a week to prevent or control a disease, I have emphasized practical alternatives suitable for small-scale home gardeners. Never, in my wildest dreams, do I see myself feeling so anxious about a disease that I would be willing to spend a half hour or more every few days messing with a sprayer. Like most gardeners, I have neither the time nor the inclination.

Environmental concerns also compel us to look at disease control strategies that do not pollute water, air, or soil. In this book, much emphasis is placed on maximizing plants' own abilities to fight disease, and on gardening methods that keep diseases in check. Chapter 1, "The Gardener as Plant Physician," gives detailed coverage of these methods, which include hot composting, crop rotation, soil solarization, and selecting the best varieties for your garden.

Some readers may use this book as a starting point for understanding the organisms that cause plant diseases, but then pursue nonorganic solutions. If you do, be sure that you read the label on any horticultural chemical twice before you unscrew the cap, and then follow instructions exactly. If you deviate from a product's prescribed use or application rate, you may burn plant leaves or cause other types of damage that are much worse than the disease you sought to control in the first place.

With the exception of the rose, the most popular perennial flower in American gardens (which happens to be closely related to brambles and many tree fruits), coverage in this book is limited to diseases that infect commonly grown vegetables and fruits. If a certain flower is frequently infected by a disease, it is mentioned in passing. But the world of flowers is so huge and global in scope that a book four times this size would be needed to give the same detail to flower diseases as is provided here for vegetables and fruits. Gardeners in search of information on confusing flower diseases may find answers in the standard horticultural reference book on the subject, *Westcott's Plant Disease Handbook*. Most major libraries have at least one copy in their reference collection.

It may seem ludicrous to think of a garden disease as leading to pleasure, but it's possible. Some of the most important decisions gardeners must make have to do with which plants to keep and which to sacrifice. The more we understand about garden diseases, the easier it is to choose plants that are likely to thrive and to provide them with the care needed to keep them healthy. And, the more satisfying it is to get rid of problem plants — without nagging questions about whether or not we did the right thing.

◄CHAPTER 1►

THE GARDENER AS PLANT PHYSICIAN
An Overview of Backyard Plant Pathology

There's no such thing as a disease-free garden. Like fleas on a dog, organisms that cause plant diseases are always present, hanging around, and waiting for a suitable host to appear. When a disease does develop, there's no single magic formula for getting rid of it. Just as a doctor can't cure all ills with an aspirin, you can't spray away all disease problems. Some understanding of the troublemaker is first required, followed by a logical, organized treatment plan.

While there are definite parallels between how doctors treat diseases that make people sick and how gardeners respond to diseases in their gardens, there also are major differences. The biggest variable is sanitation. When a disease infects a person, it does so within a closely controlled physiological system, and the doctor can intervene with specific medicines or other remedies that directly impact the organism that causes the sickness.

The situation of a plant in a garden is radically different. The garden is a dirty world, teeming with thousands of invisible microorganisms that live in soil, splash about in rainwater, or blow on the wind. It's very much an open system, in which plants are under continuous pressure to ward off threats from naturally occurring parasites. Before continuing further, let's look at the basic equipment plants bring with them to the garden world, and how they strive to protect themselves from devastating infections.

PLANT SELF-DEFENSE

When trouble threatens an animal, it can run, fly, wriggle, or swim away. Plants are destined to stay put, no matter what, and therefore have defensive talents that are quite different from those used by animals.

Most plants are composed of three basic parts — roots, stems, and leaves. Each part performs vital functions, both in terms of nurturance and defense for the plant.

Roots are usually heavily branched. This architecture serves plants well since it enables the roots to spread out through the soil to absorb moisture and nutrients and provides a reliable physical anchor for the plant. The branched design also stands ready to help the plant recover from root injuries. If a root is damaged by disease, insects, or people, the plant can quickly grow a few new root branches to make up for the lost ones.

The stem is a plant's spinal cord. The outside is made of very tough, woody, sometimes twisted cells that protect the interior. Inside, two systems of passageways known as the xylem and the phloem carry moisture, nutrients, and messages where they need to go.

If a living thing is going to spend a fruitful life in one place, it must come equipped with a protected vascular system. All mature plant stems are tough compared to the rest of the plant, but the best example is that of the tree. Tree trunks must have very hard, protective exteriors since they must safeguard the tree's vascular system for many decades.

The last and most expendable of plant parts are the leaves. You don't have to be around plants long to notice that there are tremendous differences in leaf types. They may be thick, thin, hairy, or smooth; broad or needle-thin; red, white, or green. This diversity in leaf types is one of the ways the plant kingdom keeps itself nice and confusing to insects and diseases.

Some leaf types are very difficult for anything to penetrate. Hard, shiny leaves like those of most hollies are good examples. Likewise, pine and cedar needles are unappetizing to insects and are seldom parasitized by diseases.

Most leaves of garden plants do have some weak points in their stomata, or breathing holes. These very tiny holes are used primarily to absorb and release gases, but some fungi take advantage of them and use the stomata as convenient places to anchor themselves.

Other disease organisms may enter leaves through any broken cells. Plants that have soft, fat leaf hairs, like potatoes and tomatoes, may be invaded by microorganisms when the hairs are broken by violent weather or a human touch. Other modes of entry into leaves used by disease organisms include holes made by insects or scratches made by hail.

Some organisms, notably nematodes, can directly penetrate plants and infect them. Many viruses get passed from plant to plant by insects such as aphids, thrips, and beetles. At this point you may wonder how plants manage to survive in such a hostile, pathogen-filled world. They not only survive but flourish by using physical and chemical defenses that are nothing short of amazing.

Since leaves are exposed to so many threats, it's no wonder that plants often attempt to thwart trouble by simply dropping injured or diseased leaves. When leaves fall, we often assume that the disease has killed the leaves, when in fact the disease may have caused the plant to shed its own leaves in attempt to protect itself from further injury.

Extreme drought also may cause plants to shed leaves as an act of self-preservation. They simply let go of the most expendable leaves, which relieves some of the pressure on thirsty roots. Since a plant cannot defend itself well when it is desperately short of water, this may also be a way that plants protect themselves from disease.

Certainly losing leaves weakens plants, but, except in the case of trees that are incapable of growing more than one set of leaves a year, leaf loss seldom leads to plant death. Sometimes you may notice that individual branches will become diseased and wither while the rest of the plant remains healthy. In some situations, plants can "wall off" injured or diseased parts with a chemical or physical barrier that keeps the problem from spreading to other parts of the plant.

PLANT YOUTH AND OLD AGE

The age of a plant affects how well it can protect itself from many diseases. Very young plants have tender stems that bruise easily, so they are easy prey for fungi and bacteria that specialize in colonizing succulent stems. The organisms that cause damping off are good examples. These fungi may colonize young roots or the delicate base of plants where stem changes to root. As plant tissues mature, they outgrow their susceptibility to damping off problems.

As the plants reach puberty and begin to flower and produce immature fruits, they face new challenges. The nutritional stresses of reproduction cause the plants to work at breakneck speed to keep all systems running smoothly. Leaves must photosynthesize like crazy, roots must constantly deliver moisture and nutrients, and hormones must be monitored and adjusted to keep flowering patterns on track.

Amid this organized mayhem, disease organisms may enter the picture and quickly claim a victim. Fungi that cause plants to wilt may take advantage of the plant's rapid-transit system and move up from roots to stems and clog them up. Or, organisms that get their start in damp flowers, or in pollen, may suddenly become active during the brief time that the opportunity presents itself.

After flowers and fruits have formed, the plant has fulfilled its primary mission and starts to relax. Now a new group of pathogens get their chance to establish a home. Fungi that colonize leaf stomata often have their best luck in late summer, when leaves are old and tired. As plants age they often face increased challenges from diseases. This is the way of the world, for many "natural" causes of plant death involve common diseases.

GETTING TO KNOW THE PLAYERS

The types of organisms that cause plant diseases include fungi, bacteria, mycoplasmas, viruses, and nematodes. All of these are living things that enter plant tissues and reproduce themselves. When they do, the plant hosts an infectious disease.

▲ **Fungi** are far and away the most common types of organisms that cause diseases in plants. Different fungi may infect roots, stems, or leaves, causing plants to rot, wilt, or develop leaf spots.

What are fungi? The easiest way to understand them is to think of them as microscopic organisms that parasitize plants. Fungi can be extremely small, like the genus known as Fusarium, which live inside plant roots and stems and cause fusarium wilts. Other fungi are much larger, such as those that mature into mushroomlike growths appearing on dead trees.

All common molds and mildews are fungi. If you've ever encountered moldy bread, or watched strawberries turn into balls of fuzz in your refrigerator, you've seen fungi in action.

A fungus begins its life as a seedlike spore. Many fungi are able to produce several types of spores, depending on the season. In summer, spores may have flimsy exterior walls since they live for only a few days. In fall and winter, the same fungus may switch gears and produce masses of winter spores, which are protected from weather by hard coatings. Regardless of the time of year, eliminating fungal spores is a huge challenge since there are so many of them. A small leaf spot on a tomato may easily release a thousand invisible spores.

Many of those spores will die soon after they are produced, while others will have better luck at life. When spores come into contact with a suitable host plant, they germinate. A tiny threadlike filament, called a hypha, establishes itself in plant tissue, much like a microscopic root. With this peg in place, the fungus grows by releasing enzymes that soften cell walls. More hyphae are then produced, which form a tangled spidery mass. With some other fungi, such as those that cause powdery and downy mildew, the hyphae become so numerous that you can see them on the leaves as a soft, cottony mass, called a mycelium. Within those masses are tufts of spores, which break free and blow or splash to new leaves, where their life cycle repeats itself.

There are exceptions, but most fungal spores germinate best when leaves are damp. Wet surfaces give spores the time they need to germinate without danger of drying out. Winter spores that rest in soil or plant tissue until spring often become active when warm spring rains give them the signal that the time is right to go forth and find a new home.

▲ **Bacteria** are much smaller than fungi and are very common in the wild outdoor world of the garden. Relatively few cause plant diseases, but those that do can be very difficult to control. An excellent example is the bacterium that causes fire blight of pear and apple. Insects, wind, and rain carry the bacteria to tender young twigs, where they quickly multiply and kill the twigs.

Bacteria reproduce by dividing in two. When they make their way into a suitable plant cell, they take nutrition from the cell and multiply until the plant's cell wall bursts. If conditions are right, bacteria may divide every 30 minutes or so. The numbers below show how quickly an aggressive bacterium can multiply if it finds itself in the right plant at the right time.

TRACKING A BACTERIUM'S OVERNIGHT SUCCESS

Time	Number of Bacteria
6:00 p.m.	1
6:30	2
7:00	4
7:30	8
8:00	16
8:30	32
9:00	64
9:30	128
10:00	256
10:30	512
11:00	1,024
11:30	2,048
12:00 a.m.	4,096
12:30	8,192
1:00	16,384
1:30	32,768
2:00	65,536
2:30	131,072
3:00	262,144
3:30	524,288
4:00	1,048,576
4:30	2,097,152
5:00	4,194,304
5:30	8,388,608
6:00 a.m.	16,777,216

Bacteria that cause plant diseases force their hosts to accommodate their population explosions by releasing enzymes and toxins as they grow. In this way, bacterial diseases that live inside plants, such as bacterial wilt of cucumber, are able to clog up the plants' vascular systems in only a few days, causing them to quickly wilt to death.

Fortunately, not many bacterial plant pathogens are able to survive winter in frozen soil. Therefore, bacterial diseases of plants are for the most part limited to climates where the soil rarely freezes in winter, or to bacteria that are carried through winter inside the bodies of insects. Those insects transmit the diseases to plants as they feed the following summer.

▲ **Mycoplasmas and viruses** are even smaller than bacteria. Only a few of them are aggressive enough to cause plants to quickly wilt and die. Instead, they may live inside plants all season, never actually killing them but causing all sorts of strange aberrations in plant growth. Leaves may crinkle, twist, or show bubbles of lost color as the tiny viral tidbits rob plants of their organization and divert energy to themselves. More details about viruses and larger viruslike organisms called mycoplasmas are given in Chapter 6.

Most viruses spend winter in wild host plants or the bodies of insects; they are spread from plant to plant as the insects feed. However, the insects that carry viruses are usually very small themselves. These virus-carrying insects, called vectors, typically include aphids, leafhoppers, whiteflies, and thrips. Usually only a single type of insect vector is capable of carrying and transmitting a plant virus.

▲ **Nematodes** are too small to see without the help of some magnification, but they are among the largest organisms that cause plant diseases. Often called eelworms or roundworms, nematodes resemble microscopic snakes that become plant parasites. They may live inside roots, stems, or even leaves and may survive as eggs in soil for many years. All nematodes have a needlelike appendage that sticks out of their head, called a stylet. The stylet is used to suck plant juices or to dig a hole through which the nematode can make its way inside a plant.

Nematodes that damage plants cause plenty of damage on their own, and the holes they make in plants (with their sharp stylets) become entry points for fungi and bacteria. Plants damaged by nematodes are therefore at very high risk of developing secondary infections. Chapter 7 gives more information about these interesting yet intimidating creatures and their roles in plant diseases.

Beneficial Nematodes

Not all nematodes are gardeners' enemies. Several strains have been selected for mass-production and commercial sale as a treatment for cutworms and other soil-dwelling insect pests. Instead of looking for plants to attack, these beneficial nematodes seek out habitats more to their liking, such as the bodies of Japanese beetle grubs, cutworms, root maggots, and several other pests found on or near the soil's surface. These nematodes cannot damage plants, but you will have to follow the supplier's instructions exactly to get good results with them. For example, they must be able to find appropriate prey immediately after you release them, which means you must pay close attention to timing.

THE HOST/PARASITE RELATIONSHIP

Please don't jump to the conclusion that plant diseases are so widespread and talented that your garden plants are doomed. Quite the opposite is true. While there are some diseases present in every garden, those diseases must overcome plants' self-defense mechanisms before they can flourish. General defensive tactics used by plants have already been described, but I've saved the best for last. Disease organisms require a suitable host. If the right plant isn't present, the microorganism remains dormant as long as it can, and then perishes.

Whether or not a plant is a suitable host often hinges on one of three factors. Most often, diseases cannot infect plants that are immune to the enzymes and toxins microorganisms use to establish homes for themselves. Non-host plants also are unable to provide food for the microorganism in question. Still other plants grow so vigorously that the presence of a little disease does not matter.

Most plants are immune to most diseases. Viewed the opposite way, most diseases require very specific hosts. The same strain of fusarium fungus that destroys the roots of tomatoes does not damage beans. The bacteria that cause cucumbers to wilt cannot grow inside any vegetables that are not members of the cucurbit family. Viruses that weaken raspberries are powerless in the tissues of blueberry bushes.

In addition to having their potential seriously hampered by the absence of suitable host plants, most diseases need help moving from place to place. They are utterly dependent on the forces of nature and humans for mobility. Fungal spores can blow on the wind, bacteria can be carried on the bodies of insects, and viruses can travel inside insects so tiny that they blow about like bits of ash. Nematodes can cruise to new places in rainwater or can be brought to the garden via infected transplants.

But wait. Disease organisms can only move so far in the course of their reproductive season, and geographic factors like mountains, deserts, and large bodies of water work like natural barriers in the spread of airborne pathogens. Since southern winds usually predominate in North America during the summer months (when diseases are most active), some diseases do spread northward as each year progresses. Then cold winter weather kills them off, and the airborne diseases do not appear again until southerly winds blow again the following year.

The modern nursery industry follows meticulous standards where diseases are concerned, so the chance of importing plant diseases via purchasing contaminated plants is really quite low. Organic gardeners may be offended to know that most live plants shipped across state lines are first treated with fungicides and insecticides. However, this is the only way that nursery growers can guarantee gardeners (and plant inspectors) that their merchandise is not laced with organisms that might cause diseases.

Some diseases also can be carried on seed, but again reputable dealers will never sell seed known to be contaminated. Gardeners who save seed of special varieties or trade seeds among friends must be very careful to save seeds only from plants that appear to be free of diseases. As an extra precaution, you can soak seeds for 15 minutes or more in hot (115°F=96°C) water to kill some pathogens. Immediately before planting, seeds can be doused with (but not soaked in) compost tea to inoculate them with beneficial microorganisms that might conceivably antagonize others capable of causing problems.

THE MAGIC OF ROTATIONS

Some gardeners think of plant rotation as a method used to keep plants from taking too many nutrients from the soil. By rotating crops into different spaces (tomatoes one year, beans the next, for example), you change the nature of your plants' nutrient withdrawal patterns.

While this is a very valid benefit, the importance of plant rotation to maintaining a low incidence of plant disease cannot be under-emphasized. Because diseases require the presence of specific host plants, the simple act of replacing old plants with unrelated new ones can completely thwart the progress of many diseases. This is especially true of diseases that persist in soil. Growing the favorite host of a soilborne disease organism in the same soil year after year is an invitation to disaster.

The ability to rotate crops well is a privilege of home gardening. It's one of the major differences between gardening and farming, for farmers must grow the same handful of crops year after year or risk losing their customers. Because of this economic reality, farmers have limited rotation options compared to those of gardeners. And, since gardeners can rotate most crops easily and often, we can sharply reduce disease problems by preventing easy access to preferred hosts.

COMPETENT COVER CROPS

If you take the benefits of non-host plants and crop rotations and combine them, you're getting close to a working definition of a cover crop. A good cover crop covers the surface and root zone of your soil with healthy vegetation that does not host diseases (and hopefully frustrates troublesome pathogens who are hanging around waiting for a host). When the cover crop is turned under while still green and succulent, it's called a green manure since it gives soil a big dose of plant nutrients. Dead cover crops also benefit the soil by reducing erosion and providing organic matter. Cover crops are a great way to interrupt insect and disease life cycles, improve your soil, and attract beneficial insects all at the same time.

Different cover crops work well in different climates and seasons. If you live in a dry climate, you'll probably do best with cover crops grown during the winter, when sunshine is less intense and soil moisture stays put longer. In cool, moist climates of the north, cover cropping is often most practical in late summer, after fast-maturing spring-sown vegetables have passed their prime. In the South, many cover crops can be grown during the winter or during the hottest part of summer when few vegetables grow well. When you grow a cover crop depends on which cover crop you grow. There is no such thing as a perfect cover crop for all seasons.

In general, cover crops fall into three categories: legumes, grasses, and leafy greens. Each has its place in a garden, especially when you are using cover crops to prevent or reduce problems with diseases. Here is a quick look at each group.

Legumes including clovers, beans, peas, and vetches add more nitrogen to the soil than other cover crop plants, so they are the perfect choice for "breaking in" soil that is to be used for a garden for the first time. You can choose between winter-hardy species such as crimson clover or hairy vetch and summer-hardy southern peas, soybeans, or pinto beans. To perform best, seed of most of these legumes should be inoculated with the appropriate strain of nitrogen-fixing bacteria just before you plant them (your seed source should be able to provide the right packet of inoculant powder).

To capture the maximum amount of soil nitrogen, turn under legume cover crops just as they begin to flower. In cold climates, you may be able to time your planting so that freezing weather kills your legumes at just the right time. Some legumes do host certain pathogens, including mildews and nematodes. To be safe, rotate legume cover crops with non-related edible plants such as corn, cucumber, squash, and various cabbage cousins.

Grassy cover crops include small grains such as wheat, rye, and sorghum. The greatest strength of this group of cover crop plants is the huge amount of organic matter they can provide, which improves soil drainage, tilth, and its ability to retain moisture. Some evidence indicates that grassy cover crops suppress weeds that attempt to grow just after the cover crop has been turned under.

The same wheats and rye grown for grain can be used as winter cover crops, though they are somewhat difficult to turn under unless you have a tractor with a disc. The same is true of annual rye grass, especially in mild winter areas where it is never killed by cold weather. Since grains are not closely related to any garden crop except corn, they are easy to fit into crop rotations and seldom host diseases that give gardeners trouble.

Buckwheat is not a grassy plant, but it is handled like a grassy cover crop. It's one of the most versatile of cover crops, useful for improving soil and attracting beneficial insects. Plus, buckwheat tolerates hot weather well, and is easier to turn under than other grains.

Leafy greens are ideal quickie cover crops for gardeners since they grow fast. Mustard or turnip can be ready to turn under in four or five weeks. They make good cover crop to follow tomatoes, peppers, or legumes.

All of the above cover crops can be mixed up, or you can buy cover crop seed mixtures that may include some or all of the above types of cover crops. You can mix up your own cover crop mixtures using the tail-ends of seed packets, or you can cover crop with edible varieties of beans, peas, or greens. I often dump handfuls of bush bean, southern pea, or turnip seeds into unoccupied beds, and either

Composting to Kill

Casual composting is not a cure-all for plant diseases. But hot composting, in which the temperature of the compost heap rises above 130°F (54°C) for several days, can kill most of the pathogens that give gardeners problems. Some viruses (and a few fungi) require much higher temperatures, but 130°F (54°C) is the death threshold for the vast majority of plant diseases.

Having spent much time knee-deep in compost, I can report that few compost heaps reach that temperature on their own. Personally, I have had little luck with several of the approaches widely recommended for making a heap really cook, including adding lots of manure to the heap. The magic ingredient for me is grass clippings. Many other types of green plant material may give similar results — one man I know uses chopped kudzu leaves that he mows and collects. Lots of fresh green stuff, whether grass clippings or something else, is the ingredient to add if you want your compost to get really hot.

When I have accumulated a pile of dead plants that I know are positively reeking with disease, here's what I do.

1. *When the weather is warm, I chop and mix the contaminated plant material with an equal part of mature compost. This is usually "cold compost" made from rotted leaves and kitchen waste during the winter months. When this pile is close to three feet high and three feet wide, I go looking for some grass clippings.*

To heat up a pile this size, I've found that I need about 1½ wheelbarrow loads of grass clippings, or the contents of three large

pull up the plants or turn them under when I'm ready to grow something else.

If you want to plant right away after a cover crop, pull up the plants and compost them, or use them as mulch beneath unrelated plants (for example, whole immature bush beans could be used to mulch corn). When cover crops are turned under, allow at least two to three weeks for

---

plastic garbage bags. The grass clippings must be fresh (less than five days since they were cut).

2. *It takes more than an hour to mix the grass clippings with the previously composed pile, and I keep the hose handy to gradually dampen the whole mess. When finished, the pile is quite large, but you need a big heap (a cubic yard or larger) to get the high temperatures needed to kill disease organisms.*

3. *After three days I check to see if the heap has heated up. If you don't have a compost thermometer, wrap a meat thermometer securely in plastic, and bury it in the center of your heap. Or, let your senses be your guide. A heap that is 130°F (54°C) inside feels hot to your legs when you stand beside it. If you tear it open and stick you hand in the middle, it will be so hot that you can't keep your hand in there for more than two seconds.*

4. *Three to seven days after the big heap is made, it must be turned. If the heap has not yet heated up well, this first turning should do the trick. I turn the heap again five days later so the material on the outside of the heap gets its chance in the middle (always the hottest part). After ten days to two weeks the heat falls off no matter what I do, and the compost is ready to use.*

High temperatures do most of the work, but there is evidence that the compost process kills some disease organisms by itself. Still, it's best to hot-compost plant materials you know are diseased, even if you must collect them in an isolated pile until you have the time and energy to cook them to death.

---

the plants to decompose before planting the soil with a new crop. More time may be needed, depending on temperature, rainfall, and the type of cover crop you have grown. If you need to get a cover crop out of the ground but the soil is too wet to cultivate, it can speed things along if you mow down the cover crop while you're waiting for dry weather.

In addition to rotating plants in space and time, you can help prevent and control garden diseases by maintaining biologically

Healthy Plant Checklist

At the beginning of any encounter with a garden disease, you should ask yourself questions about how the episode developed. The following checklist should help you identify contributing factors that you may be able to change.

❏ *Is the plant appropriate for your soil, climate, and the growing season? Pushing plants to grow in alien or hostile environments can increase their susceptibility to disease.*

❏ *What's the drainage situation? Normally well-drained soil can become waterlogged following frequent heavy rains, which can give rise to root rot diseases.*

❏ *Are adjoining plants affected, or only isolated plants or leaves? Small problems often can be eliminated by removing the first plants (or plant parts) to become infected.*

❏ *Did you use seeds or plants that might have carried the disease? Most reputable seed dealers sell only disease-free seeds, but seeds and plants shared among friends may not be safe.*

❏ *What plant grew in the soil before the one that is having trouble? Could it have been a host for the disease?*

❏ *How well can fresh air circulate through the plant? Is tight spacing or neglected pruning causing growth to become too crowded?*

❏ *Are other host plants living nearby?*

❏ *Is the plant old and deserving of an honorable death?*

❏ *Have you seen insects that may have transmitted the disease?*

❏ *Are varieties available that might offer some resistance or tolerance to the disease?*

active soil. When you mix vegetable waste with manure and compost it, the finished product is a banquet of ready-to-use plant foods and beneficial microorganisms. Adding this to soil has the additional advantage of improving soil structure, or tilth. Plants growing in organically enriched soil are healthier, a reflection of the balanced microbial community that you established with good soil care practices.

Choosing Resistant Varieties

Just as some species of plants are immune to attack by certain pathogens, some varieties are better able to fend off disease challenges than others. In gardening, degrees of natural disease resistance include immune, resistant, tolerant, and susceptible. Look for these words when shopping for varieties in seed catalogs. Here's what they mean:

▲ **Immune** — The organism is incapable of infecting the plant. Even when scientists put the plants in a greenhouse or growth chamber and assault them with disease organisms, they don't get sick.

▲ **Resistant** — The organism can infect the plant, but the plant can usually thwart the attack unless it is weakened by other factors such as weather damage or nematodes, or unless a new strain of the pathogen is at work. Resistant plants may block out the disease by dropping infected leaves or may not get the disease at all, even when disease pressure is severe.

▲ **Tolerant** — The organism can infect the plant but usually causes little damage. A tolerant plant may develop mild symptoms, but it has enough defensive talents to fight back. If growing conditions are very good, a tolerant plant can cross the line to resistance.

▲ **Susceptible** — The organism easily infects the plant, which defends itself weakly or not at all. In a garden, you can use susceptible plants to tell you if you have an indigenous disease.

Your responsibilities as a plant physician do not end when you choose varieties known to be tolerant or resistant to a disease that is prevalent in your area. In addition, you must do what you can to assure your plants a healthy life. Environmental factors such as poor soil drainage, poor nutrition, or strong winds that dash plants to the ground can give diseases such a boost that plants don't have a fair chance.

TREATMENT PLANS
FOR TROUBLED PLANTS

This book includes six chapters, each on a different diagnostic category (Chapters 2–8). I have organized it this way to make it simpler for gardeners to devise a good plan of intervention when a disease problem occurs. Each chapter begins with a general discussion of the type of microorganism involved in, say, soilborne diseases (Chapter 2) or viruses (Chapter 6). If you have trouble understanding the information given about a certain disease, please review the chapter's introduction.

Near the end of this book, just before the index, you will find "What's Ailing My Garden? A Quick-Reference Table to Diseases Affecting Common Garden Crops." When you see something going wrong with a plant but have little idea of what it may be, look up the plant on this table, and try to match what you see to the symptoms given. Then consult the longer entry on the disease for the detailed information you need to make treatment decisions.

If the evidence you see still does not match a certain disease, see Chapter 8, "Great Masqueraders: Common Plant Problems that Resemble Diseases," which describes insect damage and nutritional disorders that often appear to be diseases.

As you experiment with disease control strategies, don't be afraid to try new things that make sense to you. Since gardeners have time to ponder unique situations they encounter in their yards, they often come up with very innovative methods that work to control disease.

Assuming the role of plant physician can be interesting, satisfying, and fun. When you understand the diseases that reappear in your yard year after year, you can make much better decisions about what to grow where, and when, and how. My final tip to backyard pathologists is to think small. Even though diseases are mighty forces in a garden, they are tiny microorganisms. Perhaps, while pondering a mysterious blight, you will ask yourself for the first time in your life, "If I were a spore, where would I go from here?" Such questions often lead to refreshing insights on the ways of weather, nature, and the plants we love.

◄ CHAPTER 2 ►

AILMENTS FROM THE EARTH
Plant Pathogens that Live in Soil

Healthy soil is a conglomerate of small rock particles, water, spongy bits of organic matter, little insects and invertebrates, fungi, bacteria, and numerous chemical compounds. It's full of living things that are too small to see. Some of those microorganisms are capable of causing diseases in plants. This chapter is about soil-dwelling life-forms that sometimes get out of hand and make plants sick.

Dead things rot. This is the basic reality that underlies everything we know about soil. Most of the life-forms in soil are somehow involved in the process of decay, whether the dead thing in question is a plant, insect, leftovers that turned moldy in your refrigerator, or the mouse you caught under your kitchen sink and buried in your yard. If soil was not equipped to perform this vital function, the world would be swimming in its own waste.

Soil-dwelling organisms involved in this noble mission of processing dead things and causing them to decay far outnumber those that have the less-appreciated job of killing or maiming live plants. But it does make sense that such soilborne assassins should exist, for if the good-guy soil critters had to hang around all year waiting for plants and animals to die of old age, they would quite often go hungry. So the earth's soils are equipped with microorganisms that rob plants of life. The dead plants in turn become food for the microbial masses. We might call these types of organisms advance assault squads, but instead we call them diseases.

It is a very unusual soil that will not, at some time or other, give rise to a soilborne disease. More often, a garden will host several soilborne diseases capable of making plants sick. Practically every soil hosts several strains of Botrytis fungi, which specialize in making ripe fruit rot, as well as Fusaria fungi, whose job description consists mostly of turning plant roots into bits of humus.

Unfortunately, these and many other common soil diseases sometimes are not content to wait until plants are dead to attack them, so they can become problems for gardeners. It's very important to realize that some soilborne diseases are very likely to be permanent residents in our gardens.

COMPOST THERAPY

It's a dirty and diversified world out there in the ground. Communities of living soil organisms are so complex that as gardeners, we can never know with any precision just who we have living in our soil. This is where compost comes in. When dead plant parts, kitchen wastes, and manure are mixed together and dampened, they decay into a dark, crumbly mixture best thought of as essence of rot. Compost is especially rich in microorganisms that specialize in processing dead plant materials, along with the chemicals those organisms produce. When added to normal soil, compost inoculates the site with beneficial and benign soil organisms. These in turn compete with others that may cause problems.

We can get a little more specific about what goes on in compost, and how those events relate to plant diseases. When plants decompose, they are first colonized primarily by fungi. Call this Phase One. Later, when the fungi have done their job, bacteria become more active, though some fungi remain. Call this Phase Two. When compost is finished, or completely rotted, it is very rich in bacteria.

Interpreting these events a bit, we may assume that part of the bacteria's role is to subdue the fungi so that the natural succession from Phase One to Phase Two can take place. When we use compost as a preventive or follow-up therapy for soilborne diseases, we are bombarding a pre–Phase One situation (a live plant that either fungi or bacteria are trying to make into a dead one) with Phase Two performers. A top priority for these Phase Two microcritters is subjugating Phase One life-forms, many of which happen to cause diseases.

All gardeners should compost so that you will always have what you need to engage in compost therapy for troubled soil. Think of compost as a restorative health tonic for soil. Don't wait until you actually see a soilborne disease to use it, for regular applications of compost are one of the best defensive strategies you can use to keep soilborne pathogens suppressed and to promote overall vigor in plants.

If you're not careful, you may cycle disease-causing microorganisms through compost. When diseased plants are composted, the fungi or bacteria that made them sick will likely survive in decomposed plant tissue, at least for a while. Since few diseases of fruits bother vegetables, and vice-versa, it's a good idea to keep two compost piles going — one comprised of vegetable garden waste and one of fruit debris. Use the fruit debris in your vegetable soil and your vegetable compost for fruits and flowers.

Another idea is to keep a master compost heap for nondiseased plants and kitchen wastes and another for plants that die unexpectedly of disease. (See page 14 for instructions for composting diseased plants.) You should definitely avoid turning under plants that die of soilborne diseases, for this is exactly what the offending fungi or bacteria would love for you to do. For example, if your eggplant dies of verticillium wilt and you turn the plants under, you'll inadvertently sponsor a short-term fungal feast and verticillium celebration in your own garden.

Rotating crops helps keep troublesome microorganisms from going wild by depriving them of their desired host plants. But since most soilborne diseases can hang around in soil for a very long time, crop rotations by themselves are rarely capable of eliminating a disease problem.

MULCHING WITH A MISSION

Mulches can be of tremendous value when dealing with soilborne diseases. They act as a physical barrier between the soil and aboveground plant parts, often keeping disease organisms from reaching the plant parts they would most like to have. Soft mulches of chopped leaves, grass clippings, or straw also reduce the splashing that goes on when big raindrops hit the ground. Since many disease organisms travel in water droplets, the cushioning properties of mulch can slow the spread of some of these diseases.

Mulches also can help plants survive modest challenges from diseases that enter through the roots and destroy some roots in the process. If the remaining roots are able to work very efficiently, the plant may be able to produce well anyway. By keeping the soil moist, cool, and friable, mulches can be of enormous help in this struggle to survive.

Whether soil is mulched over or clean, one condition to watch for is poor drainage. Soil that dries out very slowly, either because it is in a low pocket or because the subsoil beneath it catches water like a pan, is at high risk for many soilborne diseases that thrive in soil that's really too wet for most plants. If the only place you have to garden shows questionable drainage capabilities, consider putting your garden into raised beds to counter this problem.

CURING SICK SOIL

Chemicals are available that will kill off everything that is living in soil, but this is a poor method to use in a home garden. Sacrificing beneficial soil organisms for temporary relief from a minor soilborne problem just doesn't make sense. Make no mistake: Chemical treatments give only short-term control of soilborne diseases that continue to live, unrestrained, in adjoining soil. The combination of compost therapy, crop rotation, resistant varieties, and mulching will give equal curative effects, and will last far longer than a one-shot chemical drench.

If dire measures are called for, there are two nonchemical methods that can rid soil of all life-forms for short periods of time — sterilization and solarization. Let's say you want to make your own potting soil for starting seeds or rooting stem cuttings. Seedlings and cuttings are poorly equipped to protect themselves from soilborne pathogens and may quickly rot if the potting soil is teeming with life. For these special uses, you need sterilized soil.

You can eliminate rotting risks by sterilizing the soil just before you use it. To sterilize soil, fill a metal or glass pan with loosely packed potting soil and sprinkle liberally with water. Use only old metal pans that you will never again need for baking cakes, for the damp soil may cause them to rust or corrode. Cover the damp soil tightly with aluminum foil and place in a 250°F (120°C) oven for an hour or more, or until the entire contents become steaming hot. The high temperatures and steam kill fungi and bacteria, rendering the soil sterile. Use the sterile soil as soon as possible after it has cooled. Since airborne fungal spores may quickly contaminate sterilized soil, make many small batches as you need them rather than cooking a quantity of soil at one time. Keep unused sterile soil in a tightly closed container.

If it happens to be midsummer, you can also sterilize soil mixture by placing it in black plastic pots, putting these in a cold frame or other enclosure placed in full sun, and covering the box securely with clear plastic. Let it cook for at least a week. As long as days are sunny and hot, interior heating within the box should top 130°F (65°C), the usual tolerance threshhold for soilborne diseases.

Most diseases that live in soil are increasingly prevalent toward late summer. After a long season of warm temperatures and rain you can also try solarizing individual planting beds just before you plant your fall crops. When done in mid- to late summer, when temperatures are quite warm, solarization can steam clean the top 4 inches (10 cm) of soil and thereby cause serious setbacks for all soil-dwelling plants, animals, and pathogens.

Solarizing: Step-by-Step

1. *Cultivate a plot of soil up to ten feet square (one meter square).*

2. *Add a 1- to 2-inch (2–5 cm) layer of fresh manure or slightly rotted manure and work it in well. Don't waste your compost by using it to enrich soil you're about to sterilize. Since solarization kills many weed seeds, this is a good use for weedy manures.*

3. *Shape soil into ready-to-plant beds or rows.*

4. *Dampen well and allow to settle overnight.*

5. *Spread a sheet of heavy clear plastic over the plot and bury the edges. The plastic should be somewhat loose as it will puff up with excess heat and steam. Tape up any tears or holes to keep heat from escaping.*

6. *Wait four to five weeks.*

7. *Uncover, water, and plant. Don't recultivate before planting, or you'll bring untreated soil to the surface. Some nematodes will still be present below the top 4 inches, but their numbers should be reduced to tolerable levels if you don't bring them to the surface by cultivating.*

The following mini-encyclopedia of sixteen common soilborne diseases is arranged alphabetically by common name. To find out which disease may be bothering a certain plant, consult the table in Chapter 9 (page 158).

COMMON SOILBORNE DISEASES

Blossom Blight, Wet Rot, Pod Rot

Type of Organism: A fungus classified as *Choanephora cucurbitarum*.

Host Plants: Primarily summer squash, pumpkin, and cucumber; occasionally pepper, okra, southern pea, and some flowers.

Where It Occurs: Wherever susceptible crops are grown during periods of warm, very wet weather.

Making a Diagnosis: This disease begins on flowers, causing them to decay rapidly. Blossom blight is easily identified when the fungi form fruiting bodies that look as though a thousand tiny black pins have been stuck into the blossom. This symptom occurs on both male and female blossoms. On female squash blossoms, the fruit that develops usually shows the same fungal growth as the flower, starting at the blossom end.

On okra (and its hibiscus cousins), blight may affect the blossoms but does not mar the pods. With peppers, this fungus occurs mostly on unstaked plants in which the fruits are allowed to come into contact with the ground.

Immediate Action: On all plants, clip off affected blossoms and fruits and quickly compost them. If plants are crowded, or are shaded by weeds, thin and clean the bed or row to allow sunshine to penetrate the foliage. Good air circulation is vital.

Blossom blight develops most often during periods of very rainy weather. If this weather pattern persists, clip off all blossoms to stop the progress of the disease. When dry weather returns, allow plants to flower freely.

Future Management: The fungus is a natural part of the microbial community in many soils. Where blossom blight is a recurrent problem, grow squash in raised beds and allow plenty of space between plants. Rotate plantings every year with nonsusceptible crops. Avoid overwatering squash and pumpkins. Grow cucumbers on trellises to drastically cut their risk of developing blossom blight. Stake and mulch peppers to keep them up off the ground.

Buckeye Rot

Type of Organism: A fungus, *Phytophthora parasitica* and other closely related species. A related fungus, *P. infestans,* causes a different disease known as late blight (see page 97 in Chapter 4).

Host Plants: Tomato.

Where It Occurs: Mostly in warm climates, but can occur wherever tomato fruits come into contact with soil during warm, wet weather. Spores may splash upward to fruits not touching the soil.

Making a Diagnosis: This is a soilborne disease of tomato fruits. If you don't stake or cage your tomatoes and they come into contact with the soil as they begin to ripen and turn soft, you're likely to see several different kinds of rot spots develop on the fruits. One of the more common ones is buckeye rot.

Buckeye spots are distinctive, with several concentric dark rings or bands around a dark brown center. As the fruit begins to rot, the centers of the rings may rupture.

Immediate Action: Pick off affected fruits, as they will not ripen properly or will rot right away. Stake plants to keep remaining fruits from touching the ground. If staking is impractical, mulch plants with straw, grass clippings, or another material that will form a clean blanket between the soil and ripening fruits. Or slip a folded newspaper beneath green tomatoes that are lying on the ground.

Future Management: Excellent prognosis if you grow tomatoes at proper spacing in well-drained soil and support with a stake, cage, or trellis to keep fruits from touching the soil.

Corn Smut

Type of Organism: A fungus called *Ustilago maydis*, which lives in soil and spreads by spores blowing in the wind.

Host Plants: All types of corn.

Where It Occurs: The corn smut fungus is probably native to the United States and Mexico. Outbreaks occur primarily where temperatures range between 80° and 92°F (27° and 32°C) in midsummer.

Making a Diagnosis: This disease has a very appropriate name. It disfigures sweet corn by causing the kernels to become monstrous gray and black blobs. Sometimes tassels, stalks, and other plant parts also show smutty boils, but damage is most conspicuous on the ears.

Here is how smut gets its start. Spores in soil remain viable for several years. When sweet corn plants are about three feet high, the weather becomes warm enough for the fungus to grow. Very small galls then develop on the young plants and often go unseen by gardeners. These galls release spores, which blow onto the silks of the young corn a few weeks later. The fungus then moves down into the ears. Smut fungi also may enter ears through holes in the husks made by insects or hail.

Gardeners usually notice smut when some ears begin to swell sideways two or three weeks after silks and tassels have appeared. Hugely distorted kernels may pop through the husk, revealing this ugly disease.

As awful as corn smut looks, it's considered a delicacy in Mexican cuisine. The young smutty kernels, gathered when they remain greenish white or light silver gray, are also known as maize mushrooms or Mexican truffles. The Aztec name for them is *cuitlacoche*. They have a flavor described as earthy, like mushrooms but with some corn flavor.

Although excellent plant vigor is often associated with increased resistance to disease, in the case of corn smut the opposite is true. Healthy, vigorous sweet corn may show very high rates of infection, especially when rainfall is sparse in spring and average or heavy in early summer. Another smutty paradox has to do with manure. The smut fungus passes through the digestive systems of cows and horses.

If you use this manure to fertilize your corn, smut problems may be unusually severe. Chicken manure is a safer choice for sweet corn.

Immediate Action: To reduce secondary infections, gather and destroy every smutty stalk or ear as soon as you see it. If your garden has been the site of smut in the past, learn how to feel green ears to find unusual swellings under the husk. With a little practice, you'll be able to find smut before the boils mature and release their spores. Where smut is common, plant corn as early as possible.

A few varieties are tolerant to smut. Sweet corn that develops tight husks which cover the tips of the ears offers some physical protection. Rotating corn with other crops also helps keep smut problems from increasing from year to year.

Future Management: Where smut is present, maintain constant vigilance to keep the fungus from reaching the mature stage. Over several seasons, the combination of tolerant varieties and excellent cleanliness will gradually reduce smut problems, especially if the weather cooperates with your efforts.

Crown Gall

Type of Organism: A bacterium named *Agrobacterium tumefaciens* causes this disfiguring disease.

Host Plants: Bramble fruits including raspberry and blackberry, rose, grape, fruit trees, nuts, euonymus, and perennial flowers including aster, daisy, and chrysanthemum.

Where It Occurs: In most parts of the civilized world. The bacteria can live for a year or two in soil but generally require host plants. But since most of the hosts are long-lived perennials that are often transported long distances in trucks, crown gall is constantly on the move. Persistent problems are most typical in warm climates.

Making a Diagnosis: If you conceive of crown gall as cancer of plants, you're right on target. The bacterium that causes the disease enters plants through wounds and stimulates cells to grow wildly into globular galls. As the galls swell, they interfere with the plants' abilities to move moisture and nutrients through stems. New growth is often stunted, and leaves are small with a sickly yellowish cast. In most plants, the galls are light brown to tan in color and have a corky texture.

Immediate Action: Inspect susceptible plants often so you can catch galls very early. Fill a small pail with a disinfectant solution of one part chlorine bleach to five parts water. Place sharp pruning shears or a sharp knife in this solution. Prune the plants to 2 inches (5 cm) below each gall. Swish your cutting instrument in the bleach solution between pruning cuts. Collect and burn the galls.

If the gall is at or below the soil line, as often occurs with roses, you may not be able to prune out the gall without killing the plant. In this case, dig up the plant and burn it. After digging, clean all tools in a disinfectant solution. Don't plant another rose or other susceptible plant in a spot vacated by a plant that had a gall close to the soil line.

Future Management: Gardeners used to see crown gall much more than they do today, for professionals in the nursery industry have worked very hard to eliminate it. Reputable dealers won't sell plants that are at high risk for developing this disease, and most plants that are inspected prior to interstate shipment have been screened for the presence of crown gall.

Still, crown gall is very much with us and can develop unexpectedly on plants thought to be free of the disease. Since a wound is needed to permit entry of the bacterium, use only clean tools when pruning and do most of your cutting in cold weather, when the disease is less likely to be active. Scrupulously inspect all new plants brought into your yard. Avoid buying grafted plants

Crown gall interferes with a plant's ability to move moisture and nutrients through its stems.

in which the graft union is unusually bumpy or swollen. A close cousin of the crown gall bacteria is sometimes used commercially as a root dip because it has been found to be an effective biological agent for preventing this disease. It is the newest weapon in the nursery industry's long battle with crown gall.

Cucumber Scab

Type of Organism: A fungus named *Cladosporium cucumerinum*.

Host Plants: Cucumber, squash, muskmelon, and pumpkin.

Where It Occurs: The fungus lives in many types of soils in various climates without causing problems. It tends to appear most often in cool climates where cucumbers, squash, or pumpkins have been repeatedly grown, thus giving the fungus several opportunities to flourish. Outbreaks usually occur in late summer, when nights become long and cool. Heavy dews aggravate the situation, as the fungus grows best under wet conditions with temperatures between 60° and 70°F (15° to 20°C).

Making a Diagnosis: Scab is most often seen on cucumbers. Initially the leaves develop small dark spots between veins; these are similar in appearance to those caused by angular leaf spot (see page 92 in Chapter 4).

When young fruits are infected, small sunken wet spots appear. If temperatures are well above 70°F (20°C), cucumber plants respond to the fungus by developing dark "scabs" over and around these spots. Cucumbers, squash, or pumpkins with a few scabs on them are edible but not marketable.

In cooler weather, the plants are unable to form a scab, and the spots become quite deep and begin to ooze. Frequently these fruits rot as other microorganisms enter through the diseased spots.

Sometimes scab isn't noticeable in the garden, but soft spots caused by this fungus develop when muskmelons or pumpkins are stored at cool temperatures.

Immediate Action: Whenever you grow cucumbers in late summer and allow them to run on the ground, choose a resistant variety. Most varieties that offer good resistance to downy mildew (also a problem in late summer and fall) also are resistant to scab. Cucumbers that are grown on trellises face a reduced risk from this disease since few spores reach plant parts that are several feet off the ground.

Squash and pumpkins don't get scab as badly as do cucumbers. Still, when growing these vegetables in late summer, keep plants spaced widely so that sunshine and fresh air can help keep the foliage and fruits as dry as possible.

Future Management: With cucumbers, growing resistant varieties on a trellis can virtually eliminate the risk of this disease. Good crop rotation — alternating cucurbits with unrelated plants — is also a sound preventive strategy.

To prevent scab in stored melons and hard squash, dip them in a disinfectant solution (one part household disinfectant mixed with 10 parts water) and dry thoroughly at warm room temperature before placing them in cool storage.

Damping-Off

Type of Organism: At least a dozen types of fungi that live in soil can cause young seedlings suddenly to keel over and die. When either the roots or the lower part of the stem darkens and decays, the condition is called damping-off. Among the most common culprits are *Rhizoctonia solani* (*Rhizoctonia* translates as "root killer"), *Alternaria solani*, and *Pythium debaryanum*. Sometimes more than one genus of fungus is involved in creating widespread damping-off.

Host Plants: Home gardeners frequently see damping-off of tomato seedlings, lettuce, and numerous flowers grown from seed. Virtually any seedling can be damaged by these fungi. If the tender young stem is injured in any way, permitting easy entry of fungal spores, risk of this disease is high. Sometimes beans or cucurbits sown in open soil suffer from damping-off, too.

Where It Occurs: The fungi that cause damping-off know no geographical limits. They live in all soils except those that have been recently sterilized. Artificial seed-starting mediums, such as perlite and vermiculite, rarely host these fungi. Shredded bark or sphagnum moss, added to potting soil, has been found to slow down the proliferation of the fungi that cause damping-off.

Making a Diagnosis: Damping-off can occur just as seeds germinate, causing the sprouts to rot just as they emerge from the soil. More typically, seedlings emerge and then wilt and fall over, and a small section of wet, discolored stem is easily seen just above the soil line. If seedlings become leggy because they are not getting enough light and fall over, sometimes the bent part of the stem quickly contracts the disease. When seedlings are grown in cell packs, it's not unusual for some cells to be infested with damping-off fungi, while others show no signs of disease.

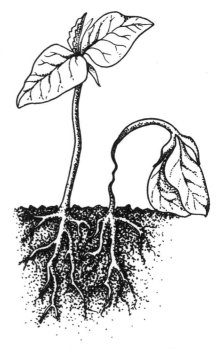

As plants grow older, the stems become resistant or immune to the organisms that cause damping-off. Once seedlings have three or four true leaves,

Damping-off causes young seedlings to die suddenly.

their physiology changes in such a way that the stem cells can no longer be weakened by the enzymes that problem-causing fungi use to gain entry. Still, a wound to the stem that breaks stem cells may provide easy access for damping-off fungi. For this reason, avoid holding the main stem of any seedling tightly or exposing the plant to strong, twisting winds that might injure it. Damping-off fungi that cause plants' roots to rot also become less threatening as the plants become older.

Immediate Action: There are many ways to prevent damping-off of seedlings. The most important strategy is to practice excellent sanitation when starting seeds indoors. Since the fungi that cause damping-off can live from year to year in the soil that clings to flats, cell packs, and other seedling containers, any reused containers should be thoroughly cleaned just before starting a new crop of seedlings.

If the containers are sturdy enough to scrub with warm, soapy water, hand washing should get them sufficiently clean. However, thin plastic containers crack easily when handled roughly. Clean them by soaking in warm water, rubbing off soil residue with your fingers, and then placing them in a large bucket. Add enough hot water to cover the containers, followed by ½ cup (140 ml) household bleach. Stir, allow to sit for a half hour or so, and then drain. Rinse well to remove traces of chlorine or other disinfectant chemicals.

In addition to cleaning your containers, you'll need to sterilize your potting soil unless you're using an unopened bagged product that is labeled as sterile. Homemade potting soil and open bags of potting soil left from previous seasons need to be sterilized before they're used for starting seeds in containers. Place a quantity in an old pan, sprinkle with water, cover tightly with foil, and bake in a 250°F (120°C) oven at least an hour, or until it's steaming hot.

Also keep in mind that most of the fungi that cause damping-off colonize living or recently deceased plant material. Special seed starting mixtures made from finely pulverized peat moss and vermiculite contain little or no food for these fungi and therefore rarely give rise to damping-off problems. If you plan to start hundreds of seedlings, it's easier and safer to buy one of these products than to sterilize a dozen batches of homemade potting soil.

Adding your best compost to soil that will be sterilized is wasteful and smelly. Compost becomes very aromatic when heated with steam, which may send you running toward the closest open windows. In addition, the assorted living organisms in compost (which include those that may cause damping-off) will be killed. Many of these organisms are beneficial when allowed to live in a natural environment, such as your garden soil. So instead of adding compost to potting soil for seedlings, use it to enhance unsterilized soil for growing older, sturdier plants.

Another tactic for cutting the risk of damping-off is to use only small containers for small plants. Since the fungi that cause the disease are nearly omnivorous, spare a single tiny plant from having to defend itself against the large numbers of hungry fungi likely to be present in a too-large container. As a general rule, keep seedlings in the smallest containers possible until roots reach the bottom and begin to cling to the sides. You can peek at them by allowing the soil to become somewhat dry and then gently tamping out the root ball. When the seedling is just beginning to become rootbound, move it to a slightly larger container.

When transplanting seedlings to larger containers, handle them by their leaves rather than the stem, since it's almost impossible to hold a young plant by the stem without bruising it. If possible, use the seedling leaves (the first ones to appear) as handles. If these leaves become injured during transplanting, the plant probably won't miss them.

Some gardeners use various chemicals to help prevent damping-off, but a word of caution is in order here. Potting soils that claim to prevent damping-off may contain fungicides that may not be approved for use with edible plants. If you decide to buy one of these products, read the label very carefully and never grow edible plants in soil intended for use only with inedible flowers.

Many vegetable seeds are treated with fungicides that help prevent damping-off while the seeds are sprouting. Treated seeds are always clearly labeled (by law) with a statement that cautions you against using them for feed or food, because they are poisonous. Birds who happen to eat them will therefore ingest poison. And, after the seeds have been rained on a few times, the fungicides leach away. Treated seed gives you no protection from the more common forms of damping-off that occur after the seeds sprout and the plants begin to grow.

Most organic certification guidelines for farmers do not permit the use of treated seeds. Fortunately, most major seed companies now sell primarily untreated seed.

If you grow mature plants in containers, they may still lose roots to some of the organisms listed here if those organisms are trapped in a flowerpot with nowhere to go and nothing to eat but your plants' roots. To minimize damage, inoculate the potting soil with a handful of good compost. As long as the plant is old enough to handle coexistence with soil microorganisms, the bacteria in finished compost can inhibit the growth of the fungi that cause roots to damp-off, or rot. In the nursery industry, growers of potted flowering plants, such as chrysanthemums and cyclamens, routinely add compost to their potting mixtures to aid in soilborne disease control.

Future Management: If you practice good sanitation in preparing seedling containers and the potting soil used to grow young plants, you'll drastically cut your risk of damping-off. In addition, healthy plants that enjoy plenty of light and good drainage will grow quickly, rapidly outgrowing the threat of this disease.

Type of Organism: Fungi. Numerous species and races of the genus *Fusarium* live in the soil and infect cultivated plants. The species name usually echoes the botanical name of the plant attacked by that particular strain of Fusarium. For example, *Fusarium oxysporum f. lycopersici* infects tomatoes, while *Fusarium oxysporum f. melonis* infects melons. *Fusarium solani* infects beans and other legumes. Collectively, this group of fungi are called *Fusaria*.

Host Plants: Various specialized Fusarium strains commonly infect asparagus, dianthus, aster, cabbage, corn, cucumber, cyclamen, carnation, gladiolus, watermelon, pea, southern pea, spinach, tomato, sweetpotato, and bean. Each strain is host specific; the same Fusarium that infects cabbage does not infect tomato. Sometimes the same species of Fusarium will occur in multiple races, as with the species that infect tomato and melon.

Where It Occurs: Fusaria are among the most widely distributed soil-dwelling fungi that attack plants. They are very common in warm climates where the soil is sandy, for these fungi proliferate best in temperatures above 80°F (27°C). However, some strains, such as those that attack beans and asparagus, thrive in the wet, cool soils of the Northwest and Northeast. Wherever you see the symptoms described below, the culprit is likely to be a Fusarium fungus. In addition to occurring naturally in many soils, Fusarium organisms may be carried from place to place on seeds and plants.

Making a Diagnosis: Two words that are commonly paired with Fusarium can be very helpful in diagnosing this disease. The first word, *wilt*, describes the tendency of infected plants to become droopy. The second word, *yellows*, describes the way infected plants often turn yellow, starting from the bottom and progressing upward, as the disease takes hold. When farmers speak of "yellows wilt" or "yellows," they usually are speaking of Fusarium. In sweetpotato, rotting stems are a common symptom.

Plants infected with Fusarium fungi wilt and turn yellow because of the way this disease operates. The spores, which are usually present in soil, enter the small fibrous roots of plants through any opening or wound in the roots. They also can enter uninjured roots. There they multiply rapidly, as most Fusaria are able to produce three different types of single-celled spores. The Fusaria quickly eat away at the small roots, rather like the athlete's foot of the plant world. These small roots rot and disappear.

At this point you may notice that plants droop even when they are well watered. Providing more water in an attempt to satisfy the needs of the plants may backfire, since many forms of Fusaria thrive in wet, waterlogged soil.

As summer progresses and the soil becomes warmer, Fusarium fungi become more numerous and aggressive. Once the small feeder roots are invaded, the disease moves into the vascular system of the plants. At this stage, yellowing of older leaves becomes evident. If the plant could talk, it would complain of constant thirst and hunger, for the disease clogs the passageways through which the plants obtain water and nutrients. Aboveground, what we see are wilted, yellowing leaves.

If you dig up an infected plant, you will find a very sparse root system and will likely see pockets of rot on the lower part of the main stem. With tomatoes, if you cut through a thick basal stem, dark streaks in the center confirm the presence of Fusarium. It strikes some plants when they are mere sprouts or seedlings, causing them to rot suddenly. On tomatoes, the damage usually becomes most pronounced just after fruit set, when there are tremendous new demands on the plants' vascular systems.

Immediate Action: Once Fusarium strikes, there is nothing you can do to restore the health of affected plants. If the disease doesn't show up until cabbages are almost ready to pick or tomatoes are almost ripe, you can certainly harvest and eat them. However, flavor and overall quality may be compromised because of the nutritional and moisture stresses caused by the disease.

When you pull up diseased plants, toss them in a burn pile or dispose of them in a special compost heap for use as mulch beneath plants that are not susceptible to the disease, such as fruits or flowers. Avoid turning under infected crops, for the disease organisms will then become even more numerous in your soil.

There are ways to work around Fusaria. Growing resistant varieties should be at the top of your list, for genetic resistance usually leads to excellent preventive control. Numerous varieties of tomato are resistant. These varieties have one or two capital Fs after the variety name. Two *F*s mean the variety resists two different races of the Fusarium subspecies that infects tomato. The same goes for melons, watermelon, and a few other plants.

If you have nematodes in your soil, even resistant plants may contract Fusarium. Nematodes make so many wounds to the roots that Fusarium fungi enter and survive, albeit with difficulty.

If resistant varieties are not available, as with beans and asparagus, some research suggests that improving soil drainage can limit Fusarium problems. Break up the subsoil, use raised beds, and never overwater plants that may be at risk.

Finally, use certified disease-free plants and seeds, and rotate plantings as best you can so that Fusarium fungi have limited opportunities to build up in your soil. Planting the same thing in the same soil year after year can create Fusarium problems where once there were none. In the late 1980s, some Peruvian coca farmers blamed their failed crops on drug agents. The real cause was a new strain of Fusarium that had emerged after several years of continuous cropping with coca.

Future Management: You will never get rid of any strain of Fusarium that calls your soil home — even with no host plants present, some strains have been known to persist for fifteen years! Using strategies that keep Fusarium problems from developing or increasing are always worthwhile. If any strain of Fusarium is common in your area, grow resistant plants or varieties to avoid serious damage.

Gray Mold, Botrytis   *bow-tri´-tis*

Type of Organism: A large group of fungi, probably comprised of several species, known collectively as *Botrytis*. Gray mold is also called botrytis blight or botrytis fruit mold.

Host Plants: Berries, especially strawberry, blackberry, highbush blueberry, and grape; lettuce, bean, asparagus, and occasionally tomato; and numerous flowers, especially tulip and others with thick, succulent petals.

Where It Occurs: Worldwide. Most problematic in cool, humid regions as the Northeast and Northwest.

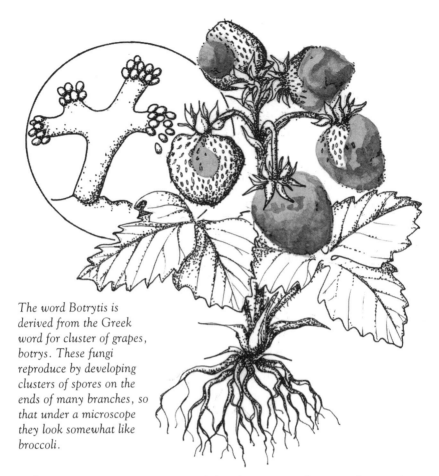

The word Botrytis is derived from the Greek word for cluster of grapes, botrys. These fungi reproduce by developing clusters of spores on the ends of many branches, so that under a microscope they look somewhat like broccoli.

Making a Diagnosis: Perhaps you didn't know it at the time, but you've seen botrytis. It's the furry coating on the soft strawberries found in the middle of a pint package. On mulch, it's the cottony white mold that develops during periods of cool, damp weather.

Botrytis is everywhere, for it is one of nature's leading rotters of recently deceased plant material. Unlike some fungi, botrytis is favored by cool conditions, as evidenced by the fresh blackberries you put in your refrigerator, only to find them moldy two days later.

In some places, such as the cool humid Northeast, botrytis can be quite troublesome for gardeners. However, in most areas this disease does not bother healthy plants. Many times I have watched it move from mulch to cucumber vine and not cause any problems. But if you live where the weather stays constantly cool and moist, watch out for this disease, especially in spring and late summer.

Fermented Compost Tea

Botrytis mold is one of several diseases that can be overpowered by the beneficial bacteria present in fermented compost tea. Scientists in Germany and Israel have found that when properly made, fermented compost tea (also called watery compost extract) can reduce the severity of botrytis molds, tomato early and late blights, and downy and powdery mildews by 50 to 90 percent.

The scientists believe that compost tea works by boosting plants' natural defenses and by suppressing the growth of the troublesome fungi. In the presence of recently applied compost tea, fungal spores germinate but then fail to develop hyphae (the fungal equivalent of roots and branches). If you apply compost tea to a badly infected plant, it will not kill fungi that already are established in leaves, but can slow the spread of the disease to other leaves. To make compost tea:

1. *Mix one part mature compost that includes some rotted manure (horse, cow, or chicken) with five parts water. A plastic milk jug works well.*

2. *Allow the mixture to sit and ferment in a shady place for ten days to two weeks. The effectiveness of the tea is highest when the tea ferments for a full two weeks.*

3. *Filter the mixture through cheesecloth to remove large particles. Do not attempt to remove all residue, for some residue gives the tea*

In a vegetable garden, the most common casualties of botrytis are lettuce and endive. If they are in a wet place and closely spaced, the disease can quickly develop in the area below the outer leaves. If crowded seedlings are rapidly shriveling and dying, check the base of the plants for deposits of gray mold.

Asparagus beds that are heavily mulched with compost or manure also may show gray mold when the shoots are just poking through in early spring. Cool, wet weather in late winter sets the stage for this damage.

Gray mold is best known on fruits, especially berries. Strawberries lying on unmulched ground, in direct contact with soil, are at very

*extra disease-fighting punch. Warning: This stuff can smell terrible —
do your straining outdoors! The odor does vary from batch to batch.*

4. *If needed, you can dilute the tea with more water, but keep the
mixture at half strength, minimum.*

5. *Either spray on leaves with a pump or pressure sprayer, or
dribble it on with a watering can. Coat both sides of leaves.*

6. *Reapply after two to three weeks.*

7. *The residue left after the tea is strained may be poured out on
the ground below plants.*

*In addition to fighting foliar diseases, compost tea can provide
some nutrients to plants, especially if they are stressed (stressed
plants are more likely to uptake nutrients applied to leaves). The
pH of compost tea is normally high — around 8.0 — which may
be an added benefit if your soil is naturally acidic.*

*As with any water-based spray, do not apply the tea to plants
when the sun is blazing since it may damage leaves. However, my
own experiments have shown that the tea itself has no ill effects
when properly applied to a variety of vegetable crops — tomatoes,
peppers, beans, peas, and others.*

*If you apply the tea to plants whose fruits are ready to harvest,
be sure to wash the food well before you eat it. After all, you are
applying a teeming community of bacteria and fungi to what you
are about to put in your mouth.*

high risk. Plus, as soon as any berries are picked and chilled, Botrytis
fungi become active. The fungi produce enzymes that soften the
tissue, so at first you may see only soft, bruised areas. But within one
to two days, fuzzy mold develops on the fruits.

Immediate Action: With lettuce, thin plants right away and lightly cultivate the soil where plants stricken with gray mold were grown. Sunshine
and fresh air are strong deterrents for gray mold.

On asparagus (and peonies and tulips), avoid mulching over the
plants with thick layers of compost or manure, unless you can do it in

late fall so that the material is totally rotted by spring. Instead, use a thin top-dressing of manure, topped with straw. In early spring, rake the mulch from the beds to expose emerging buds to sunshine. Keep the mulch piled nearby in case you need it for late freeze protection.

Strawberries are less likely to become moldy before their time if the plants are mulched with pine needles or rotted leaves, both of which make a poor medium for botrytis fungi. If botrytis is a constant problem with strawberries, try treating the plants with a baking soda spray weekly, or fermented compost tea every two weeks, beginning just after fruit set. (To make baking soda spray, mix one teaspoon per quart of water.) Lay folded newspapers beneath fruits that lie on the ground.

Botrytis can be difficult on raspberries, which mature while nights remain cool in many climates, and on blackberries grown in the Northwest. If gray mold is a yearly problem, begin applying fermented compost tea to the berries when they are green, and repeat every two weeks.

If fermented compost tea does not work, you can move on to stronger natural fungicides, including lime sulfur, copper, copper sulfate, or bordeaux mixture. Leaf injury is a constant threat with these fungicides, so follow label directions exactly and apply them when the weather is right — ideally very early in the morning on a sunny day. These fungicides are most valuable if you have a large planting and the weather forecast calls for more cool, wet weather. In a home garden, careful pruning out of old berry canes and trellising to keep the fruiting canes high above the ground drastically reduce the risk of Botrytis problems.

Future Management: Very good, especially if you are willing to accept that botrytis fungi merely do their job, which is to help old things rot. This fungus rarely attacks healthy plants growing under good conditions.

Pink Root

Type of Organism: A fungus named *Pyrenochaeta terrestris*.

Host Plants: All members of the onion family; particularly troublesome on bulb onion and scallion. Leek and chives are resistant, but not immune, to pink root.

Where It Occurs: This very widespread and long-lived soil inhabitant can occur anywhere, but it is most common in places where onions are often grown.

Making a Diagnosis: The pink root fungus attacks onion roots, causing them to rot. As more roots die, the plants appear stunted. If you dig up a plant stricken with pink root, the remaining roots will have a distinctive pink color. Healthy onion roots are white, so it's easy to tell the difference.

Sometimes the disease doesn't become severe until onions develop bulbs. Infected bulbs are soft and small. Below the bulbs, pink roots are evident.

Immediate Action: Pull up infected plants and fill the vacated furrow with good compost. Pink root fungi can survive in the soil for six years or more, so it's important to administer first aid to keep the fungus from proliferating after the host plants are removed. The myriad bacteria and fungi in compost may seriously slow the progress of the fungus. Well-drained soil that is amply endowed with organic matter also discourages this disease.

Once pink root has appeared in a garden, mark the spot and do not grow onions there again. If your whole garden space seems to host this disease, solarize soil immediately before planting onions and grow only resistant varieties.

Future Management: Because pink root is so persistent in soil, don't tempt fate by growing susceptible varieties in soil known to be infected. Several varieties of bunch onion, or scallion, are resistant, and some bulb onions are tolerant.

In addition to choosing varieties carefully, good soil maintenance can go a long way toward managing this disease. Use plenty of compost when preparing the soil for onions, and always grow onions in a deeply dug, well-drained site.

Red Stele

Type of Organism: A fungus classified as *Phytophthora fragariae*.

Host Plants: Strawberry, loganberry.

Where It Occurs: In northern states and all cold climates where the soil remains wet and cold from fall to late spring.

Making a Diagnosis: Strawberries afflicted with red stele lose most of their roots to this devastating fungus, which thrives in cold, wet soil. The word stele (pronounced *steel'-ee*) means the interior vascular pipeline inside the root. When you dig up a plant with red stele, most of the side roots will have rotted away, and the ones that remain will show reddish coloring in the stele or surrounding cortex. Slice the roots open and take a look.

Before the disease gets this far, other symptoms may appear on the plants. Usually the disease develops in plantings that have been in place for several years, though it may turn up on new plantings when diseased plants are used. At first, as small feeder roots are destroyed by this root-rot fungus, old leaves begin to dry up and wither, and new leaves are produced with little enthusiasm. As more roots are destroyed, new leaves may take on a bluish cast, flowering and fruit set is minimal, and plants suffer greatly from any drought. Badly diseased plants die when so few roots exist that they can no longer uptake sufficient water and nutrients to keep the plants alive. Because this disease spreads quickly from plant to plant in wet soil, entire rows or fields may succumb to red stele.

Immediate Action: Turn under sick plants and abandon the site as a strawberry habitat for at least ten years. Even without host plants present, this fungus can persist in soil for a decade. Except for loganberry, which is susceptible to at least one strain of red stele, the space may be replanted with fruits other than strawberries, or with vegetables or flowers.

Establish a new strawberry patch using resistant varieties, and locate the new planting where rainwater from the old planting site will not wash in. The fungus is easily spread by water that flows both above and below ground. Some red stele spores can even move about in search of host roots.

Future Management: If red stele is common in your area, grow only resistant varieties and move your strawberry patch to new soil every four or five years. This preventive rotation may help keep the red stele fungus from building up, especially if you start with disease-free plants each time around. In addition, you will thwart many other diseases that bother strawberries.

Scurf

Type of Organism: A fungus named *Monilochaetes infuscans* causes scurf in sweetpotatoes. A similar fungus, *Spondylocladium atrovirens*, causes scurf of regular potatoes.

Host Plants: Sweetpotato and potato.

Where It Occurs: In all areas where either type of potato have previously been grown. Gardeners also may import scurf by using contaminated seed potatoes or plants.

Making a Diagnosis: On both sweetpotatoes and potatoes, scurf is a disease of the skin. It turns pretty potatoes ugly, though they may still be eaten — at least for a short time after harvest. Because the skin of infected tubers can't do its job of keeping moisture in, they don't store well and often are the first to shrivel and become pithy.

When potatoes or sweetpotatoes have scurf, there are no symptoms on the plants. The crops grow normally, and you won't notice a problem until the roots or tubers are dug, washed, and set to cure.

On sweetpotatoes, scurf begins as small brown spots that expand until much of the tuber appears to have been painted with blackish brown dye. Since the discoloration is actually a part of the skin, it can't be rubbed off. The flesh beneath scurf-stricken sweetpotatoes appears normal.

On regular potatoes, scurf is often called silver scurf, since it causes light brown scabby places that eventually turn a silvery color. As with sweetpotatoes, the flesh beneath the scurf appears normal.

Immediate Action: Scurf fungi can live in soil for short periods of time, yet to persist they require the presence of host plants. If you find yourself harvesting potatoes with scurf, keep in mind that each little tendril of root left behind in the soil probably hosts this disease. For this reason, you'll need an extra-long rotation period to grow scurf-free potatoes in that spot.

You can eat potatoes marked with scurf, but do not use them as seed. Any apparently scurf-free potatoes grown in the same place and time as others that show the disease probably are contaminated.

If scurf is an unusual problem in your area, you probably imported the fungus with your seed potatoes or sweetpotato slips. To avoid future problems, purchase certified disease-free planting stock. As an extra precaution, snip off the bottom half inch of sweetpotato slips before planting them, for this is the part most likely to house the scurf fungus.

Future Management: Scurf of white potatoes is easier to eliminate than scurf of sweetpotatoes. By rotating crops and using disease-free seed potatoes, you can manage scurf into oblivion.

The fungus that causes scurf of sweetpotatoes is more persistent in soil, especially in climates with mild winters where sweet potatoes often are grown. In addition to living in the soil, scurf can spread through organic matter, rainwater, or on contaminated tools and containers. The good news is scurf must have sweetpotato tissue or eventually it will perish. Long rotations coupled with the exclusive use of disease-free slips can really slow down this disease. If your soil is naturally acidic, don't apply lime to soil destined to be planted with sweetpotatoes, as a slightly acidic pH may discourage this disease.

Soft Rot, Watery Rot, Lettuce Drop, Stem Rot

Type of Organism: Several species of *Sclerotinia*, which are common soilborne fungi.

Host Plants: Bean, cabbage family, carrot, celery, cucumber, eggplant, lettuce, onion, potato, pepper, squash, and tomato, plus numerous flowers including delphinium and peony.

Where It Occurs: This fungus may establish itself anywhere. It causes problems mostly in moist, cool climates, in soil that is not very well drained and low in organic matter.

Making a Diagnosis: The symptoms of soft rot vary with the crop affected. In lettuce, plants fail to grow well and outer leaves begin to shrivel. Beneath the outer leaves, a white cottony mold develops. As the mold moves into the plant centers, they flop over and die. The same process occurs with cabbage-family crops, which become very smelly as the rot progresses. On carrot, the tops of the roots begin to rot, leaves turn yellow and die, and cottony patches of mold develop along the soil surface. On celery, this disease is called pink rot. It normally strikes in late summer or fall, or in spring on celery grown in mild-winter areas. The mature plants suddenly turn pinkish brown, with traces of cottony white mold, and then fall over and rot.

On most other crops, soft rot establishes itself more slowly and is usually limited to infections in stems. With all plants, the ultimate evidence of soft rot appears after the plants are thoroughly infected. As it matures, the soft rot fungus forms black chunks (sclerotia) that look like mouse droppings imbedded in the plant tissue. The chunks are round or oblong and about the size of peas.

On tomato, the evidence of soft rot is more of a dry rot that girdles the lower stems closest to the soil. The stems become covered with a white, dry rot. The black sclerotia may be imbedded inside the stems or appear in splits or breaks that develop in diseased tissue.

If temperatures are between 60° and 65°F (15° and 18°C) and the humidity is high, these black chunks develop little mushroom-like appendages that are filled with spores. The stems of the mushrooms may be from ½ inch to 3 inches (1–8 cm) long. At temperatures above 80°F (27°C), the fungus becomes inactive. However, the fungus can grow when temperatures are as low as 40°F (4°C). The little black bundles can survive buried in soil for more than five years.

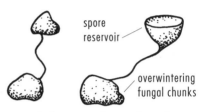

In cool, damp weather, soft rot fungi develop fruiting bodies that resemble mushrooms. They grow out of the black pealike structures.

If you're not quite sure the disease you're seeing is soft rot, take a diseased plant and place it in a cool, humid place to continue rotting. Within a week you should see either the little black chunks or mushroomlike fruiting bodies. The black chunks are more common, for the primary survival strategy of this fungus is to overwinter as mouse-dropping look-alikes and then to develop fruiting bodies when the temperatures are just right in spring.

Immediate Action: Most of the things you do to grow a healthy garden will discourage soft rot fungi. Improving the drainage and organic matter content of the soil, growing healthy plants at wide spacings, and deeply cultivating the soil before planting can make a huge reduction in the severity of this disease.

Home gardens are often poor habitats for these fungi, for home gardeners usually rotate plantings. If your garden seems to have more than its share of soft rot fungi living in the soil, consider going to raised beds. With lettuce, emphasize upright varieties such as romaines in place of those that spread their leaves over the ground.

When disease outbreaks occur, do not turn under the sick plants. If the dark pealike structures are present, they will wait patiently in the soil for years until another host appears. Instead, burn plants or chop plants into a hot compost heap (see page 14). Use that compost beneath fruits or trees, or sterilize it and use it in potting mixtures.

If you know some of these fungi are hanging around in soil, use compost freely in that spot. The bacteria in compost are believed to inhibit the germination of soft rot spores.

Future Management: Once this fungus has established itself in your soil, you can never again be lax when it comes to soil maintenance chores. Grow plants that grow up rather than out, such as romaine lettuce in place of butterheads, or broccoli in place of cauliflower. Keep carrots in well-drained raised beds. With larger plants, black plastic mulch can reduce soft rot problems since it forms a physical barrier between the plants and the soil.

If nothing seems to work, there is a chance that you can rid the top few inches of soil from these (and other) fungi via solarization. See page 23 for instructions.

Southern Bacterial Wilt

Type of Organism: A strain of bacteria named *Pseudomonas solanacearum*.

Host Plants: Tomato, potato, pepper, eggplant, and occasionally bean, root crops, and flowers.

Where It Occurs: Southeastern United States and other tropical and subtropical climates. Southern bacterial wilt is absent where the ground freezes repeatedly in winter, or where soil is extremely acidic.

Making a Diagnosis: This mysterious disease usually strikes in midsummer, when temperatures range in the 80s and 90s. Plants wilt more than usual at midday and recover overnight, but each day the wilting becomes worse and worse, no matter how much you water. Since the disease doesn't travel from plant to plant except through soil, it's not unusual for individual or closely spaced plants to become afflicted, while others only a few feet away escape infection.

By the time you decide that an infected plant is sick, the disease will have spread through the base of the plant. Cut open a large stem, and a dark ring will show in the plant's vascular system. The disease will have poisoned and clogged the passageways whereby the plant usually gets water, so much so that heavy watering will have little effect.

Infected plants usually die within two weeks. Stricken tomatoes wilt to death more quickly from this than they do from Verticillium or Fusarium wilts. Usually the leaves don't turn yellow. By the time the plant dies, the stems may have become unusually soft and mushy.

Potatoes also may develop soft stems, and the tubers often show an interior brown halo when cut open.

Immediate Action: Pull up affected plants and compost them when you diagnose this wilt for they will not be able to recover. Any new growth they manage to produce will be dwarf or weak, because the plants are in a state of nutrient starvation.

Toss a shovelful of compost into the hole where you pulled up the plant. The assorted fungi and bacteria in compost will launch a microbial war on the bacteria and hopefully overtake the troublemakers.

The bacteria that cause southern bacterial wilt live in soil for five years or more, often very deep in the soil. It is probably a common member of your soil's microbial community if you live anywhere between Maryland and Texas. Keeping the bacteria suppressed requires crop rotation, regular enrichment of the soil with compost, and use of healthy plants.

Future Management: Southern bacterial wilt takes victims from time to time but generally doesn't cause gardeners big problems. Its appearance is very unpredictable, especially in soil that supports constantly changing plants. If you live in an area where this bacteria is found in soil, sooner or later you may lose a plant or two. But with this disease you may feel thankful that it wasn't something worse.

Southern Blight

Type of Organism: A fungus classified as *Sclerotium rolfsii*.

Host Plants: Primarily pepper; tomato, bean, sweetpotato, peanut, southern pea, and melon.

Where It Occurs: Subtropical and tropical climates, including the Southeastern United States.

Making a Diagnosis: This fungus lives on bits of dead plant material in the soil, yet it is capable of suddenly killing large pepper plants if conditions are exactly right. Temperatures must be between 85° and 95°F (30° and 35°C) for several days, with light, intermittent rainfall.

When the fungus attacks a pepper plant, the plant wilts quite suddenly and a white, cottony ring (the fungi's mycelia) forms a collar around the plant's main stem, right at the soil line. Thus girdled by the fungus, the plant quickly dies. Only one or two plants may become sick, while the others remain healthy.

Immediate Action: In most gardens southern blight is an occasional problem that is usually prevented by rotating peppers with unsusceptible crops. If peppers or tomatoes must be grown in the same spot two years in a row, it may help to cultivate frequently around the base of plants to keep the soil disturbed. In midsummer when conditions favor the fungus, drenching pepper plants with compost tea will inoculate the soil beneath your plants with bacteria and fungi that may compete with the offending strain. Pull out infected plants to limit the proliferation of this fungus. Sclerotia also can persist on fallen leaves below the plant. Dispose of infected plants and mulch in a hot compost heap (see page 14).

Future Management: The fungus that causes southern blight is probably present in any soil that receives regular additions of organic matter in a warm, subtropical climate. In many ways it is a beneficial fungus since it is known to be omnivorous where dead plant material is concerned. Pepper and tomato are the most common plants it infects. Since damage is usually limited to a few plants (at most), simply growing a few extra peppers, in anticipation of possible casualties, is a wise move. Seed catalogs do not usually mention resistance to this disease, but peppers do vary in how well they can stand up to southern blight. Sweet Banana is known to be susceptible, while California Golden Wonder is highly resistant. In your garden, keep records of which varieties fall prey to this disease and avoid growing them again.

Texas Root Rot

Type of Organism: A fungus named *Phymatotrichum omnivorum* causes this devastating disease. The species name, *omnivorum*, provides a hint as to the wide range of possible host plants, which exceeds 1,700 different species.

Where It Occurs: The range is limited to Texas and adjoining corners of Louisiana, Oklahoma, and Arkansas. Some soils in the Four Corners area of Arizona, Utah, Nevada, and California also are infested. The fungus grows best in heavy, alkaline soils that are low in organic matter.

Host Plants: Texas root rot is sometimes called cotton root rot because cotton is highly susceptible. Most fruits, annuals grown in summer, and numerous vegetables also are susceptible. The list of known resistant plants is shorter than the list of susceptible ones.

The following common garden plants are thought to be resistant to Texas root rot:

alyssum	lily	pumpkin
amaranth	mints	sage
basil	*Monarda*	snapdragon
California poppy	muskmelon	stock
candytuft	mustard	strawberry
canna	nasturtium	strawflower
cucumber	oxalis	verbena
daffodil	pansy	violet
dill	petunia	wallflower
fennel	phlox	watermelon
foxglove	pomegranate	yucca
gypsophila	portulaca	zinnia
iris		

Making a Diagnosis: This disease begins its most active period in mid-summer, and new casualties continue until frost. It lives in the soil all year but doesn't spread much until soil temperatures become quite warm. Then, large or small circles of plants may suddenly wilt and die within a period of days. If rainfall follows such an outbreak, mats of spores that resemble pancake batter may appear on the soil's surface.

As these mats mature, they become powdery with millions of spores. Sometimes yellowish to tawny brown growth covers diseased vegetables and flowers. Once an outbreak is under way, it spreads rapidly, often killing all susceptible plants within 30 feet.

Immediate Action: Some gardeners will have luck stopping the spread of Texas root rot by applying ammonium sulfate (a standard inorganic fertilizer) to the soil around plants. This has a shocking effect on pH and thereby reduces the ability of the fungus to prosper. The usual rate is 1 pound per 10 square feet (0.5 kg per square meter). This is worth a try on valuable fruit trees and shrubs. Although it's not a strictly organic method, it may be your only hope. For the method to work best, the ammonium sulfate must be thoroughly watered in, usually by soaking the plant's root zone twice a week for two weeks. Prune back the top of the plant to reduce moisture stress and promote recovery.

A much better strategy is to work on preventing the proliferation of the fungus. Intensive manuring, frequent use of compost, and other methods such as cover cropping (see pages 12–16) that boost the soil's organic matter content can go a long way toward protecting vegetable and flower gardens. The assorted types of bacteria and fungi found in compost and manure compete with Texas root rot fungi and make it much more difficult for the bad guys to take over.

When planting long-lived fruit trees in this disease's geographical range, a huge planting hole should be dug and backfilled with rich, organically active soil. Planting fruit trees in unimproved alkaline clay is an invitation to disaster. Many orchardists test their soil for root rot by planting a crop of cotton first. If the cotton becomes diseased, they know to look for a better place to plant orchards.

In all areas where Texas root rot is present, try to rotate susceptible crops with resistant ones in summer plantings. Or, grow susceptible vegetables in spring and early summer and resistant ones in late summer and early fall. Since members of the cucumber family are resistant, they should be prominently represented in vegetable gardens.

You should also emphasize winter-hardy vegetables. In the areas where Texas root rot occurs, winter weather is mild enough for growing hardy and half-hardy vegetables such as cabbage and its relatives, parsley, carrots, and others that like cool weather.

As is apparent from the preceeding list of resistant plants, many of the flowers that are resistant grow in fall, winter, and early spring when the disease is inactive. In summer, use resistant plants as much as you can. In addition to the flowers listed, many native wildflowers are resistant to this disease.

Future Management: If you garden where Texas root rot is known to be present, every gardening decision should include some thought of this disease. Improving soil structure, moderating the pH, and continuously enhancing the microbial diversity of your soil should be ongoing processes.

Verticillium Wilt   *ver-te-sil´-ee-um*

Type of Organism: A fungus, *Verticillium albo-atrum*, and several other closely related species.

Host Plants: Eggplant and tomato are highly susceptible; pepper and potato also may get the disease, but they are not as seriously damaged as eggplant and tomato. Strawberry and numerous weeds serve as alternate hosts.

Where It Occurs: Various races of Verticillium are widely distributed throughout most of the United States and other temperate and semi-tropical areas of the world. Long periods of cool, moist weather with temperatures in the low 70s (around 20°C) favor the development of this fungus. It is not a serious problem in the warm Southern states with acid soils.

Making a Diagnosis: Verticillium fungi enter roots through any small breaks they encounter. In susceptible plants, they establish colonies inside the roots and lowest stems, clogging them so that moisture and nutrients can't reach the higher parts of the plant.

The first symptom, midday wilting, is soon followed by prolonged droopiness that doesn't respond to supplemental watering. The leaves usually wilt without first turning yellow, distinguishing this disease from Fusarium wilt. Eggplant is extremely susceptible, and young plants may wilt to death quickly. In badly infested soil, eggplant transplants often die within a month after they are set out in late spring. With tomatoes, wilting usually becomes most pronounced just after the plants have become loaded with green fruit.

With badly wilted tomato plants, you can also look at the insides of lower branches for evidence of verticillium. Dark streaks will be present, as if dirty water had been pumped through the plant's vascular system. Where root-knot or other nematodes are present, verticillium damage may be fast and severe, since the nematodes provide numerous openings through which the fungus can enter plant roots.

Immediate Action: With eggplant, pull up the diseased plants and dispose of them outside the vegetable garden. Since no resistant varieties are yet available, current options are: 1) Grow eggplant in containers filled with sterilized soil, kept up off the ground to protect them from contamination, or 2) Graft eggplant onto a resistant tomato rootstock. This grafting is as tricky as any grafting, but it's worth a try if you love eggplant and are interested in an adventuresome experiment.

If tomatoes contract Verticillium wilt just as the fruit is getting ripe, you can eat those tomatoes, but don't save the seeds. Also, you'll want to get the plants out of your garden as soon as possible to keep the fungi from multiplying. Once infected, plants cannot recover. As the plants become sicker, they won't be able to pump nutrients to ripening fruits, and the fruits will shrivel.

Resistance to verticillium wilt in tomatoes is controlled by a dominant gene. Since the late 1960s, this gene has been bred into hundreds of varieties, both hybrid and open-pollinated. Where you suspect Verticillium is present, choose a resistant variety (the letter V will appear after the variety name). If you must grow a non-resistant heirloom tomato where soils are infested, the safest strategy is to keep plants in containers filled with sterilized soil.

Peppers and potatoes seldom die from Verticillium wilt, but the disease can weaken them while using them as hosts. Since tomatoes, eggplants, peppers, and potatoes all are members of the same family (Solanaceae), they should be grouped together for rotation purposes. In gardens with Verticillium, observe three-year rotations with all the Solanaceaous plants.

Future Management: Verticillium fungi are naturally occurring, well-adjusted members of the soil's microbial community in many areas. You can't get rid of the disease forever, but you can suppress populations by encouraging competing microorganisms through adding compost, cover cropping, and crop rotation.

◄ CHAPTER 3 ►

MOBILE MARAUDERS
Airborne Pathogens that Persist in Host Plant Tissues

Some of the most common plant diseases in any yard are those that can live from year to year in living or dead plant tissues and also can spread by blowing on the wind. These guys have it made, survival-wise. All they need for a happy life is a plant to live on, and they can wait patiently in seeds, dead stems, or the bark of a tree until one appears. I call them mobile marauders since they can move about in so many ways: carried in a wheelbarrow full of dead plants, spread around in mulch materials, transported across the country in seed packets, or wafted about on summer breezes or in droplets of wind-blown rain from plant to plant or garden to garden.

Mobile marauders sound scary, and they are. Brown rot can mummify peaches and plums; powdery mildew can sap energy from a wide range of plants including cantaloupe, phlox, and zinnia; and anthracnose fungi can cause ugly sores on dozens of garden plants.

Most of the diseases discussed in this chapter are caused by fungi, while a few are caused by bacteria. Some particularly aggressive fungi, such as those that cause powdery mildew and downy mildew, are able to penetrate healthy leaves and establish themselves. Others do better if they find some type of opening. Fruit rots caused by fungi often enter through the tiny feeding holes insects make.

Commercial growers often use fungicides to protect plants from these diseases. But to be effective, the fungicide usually has to be maintained as a continuous film over leaf surfaces. If you live in a rainy climate, where the fungicide is constantly being washed off, you often need to reapply the chemicals more than once a week.

Few gardeners want or need to go to this trouble. Besides, fungicides don't always work. I know of many fruit farmers who have lost their crops to these diseases in bad years despite intensive spray schedules. And some diseases of vegetables, such as early blight of tomato, simply do not respond to fungicide treatment. Instead of promoting fungicide dependence, I have sought out and emphasized control measures that are most suitable for gardeners with a modest-sized planting to protect. Of particular importance is compost tea, which is described in detail on page 38.

The following mini-encyclopedia of fifteen common mobile diseases is arranged alphabetically by common name. To find out which disease may be bothering a particular plant, consult the table in Chapter 9 (page 158).

COMMON AIRBORNE DISEASES

Anthracnose   *an-thrak'-nos*

Type of Organism: A large group of fungi primarily consisting of *Colletotrichum* species. Different species infect different plants. Those that infect beans and cucurbits occur in several different races.

Host Plants: Most important on bean, cucumber family (especially watermelon), rose, grape, and bramble fruit. Causes occasional problems on potato, turnip, snapdragon, pea, grain crops, and annual flowers. Occasionally spinach and other leafy greens suffer wet leaf spots from this disease, but damage is usually very light.

Where It Occurs: Anthracnose travels easily on seed, yet depends on wet weather to help it spread through a garden. Infected seed can cause young plants anywhere to be diseased. However, the disease occurs most often in humid climates where summer rainfall is frequent and prolonged. Anthracnose is rare in dry, arid climates.

Making a Diagnosis: The word *anthracnose* derives from two Greek words meaning "ulcer disease." Its main symptoms are dark, raggedly circular, often sunken wet spots on leaves, stems, and fruits. However, the exact appearance of the disease varies with the affected crop. The following discussion will acquaint you with its most common faces.

Bean and Potato. Beans that are infected very early, or are grown from infected seed, often die soon after they sprout. The symptoms are similar to damping-off, as the anthracnose ulcers usually girdle the plants' main stems just above the soil line. The anthracnose species that infects beans is most active when temperatures are around 60°F (15°C). Anthracnose damage to potatoes is similar; it tends to be most evident on the stems near the soil line.

In addition to being introduced to the garden on contaminated seed, bean anthracnose can persist in dead plants. The fungus has a hard time surviving in soil from one year to the next but usually finds sufficient hosts to remain present throughout a growing season.

In beans, anthracnose is typically spread by wind-driven rain. The spores are equipped with little sticky organs that enable them to paste themselves to damp bean plants. During a gusty thunderstorm, these spores may be blown 20 feet or more.

Bean anthracnose also may be spread by gardeners working among wet bean leaves. Most water droplets from infected plants contain the fungus, which is easily transferred to any wet leaf a gardener happens to touch.

With beans grown from clean seed, bean anthracnose is most easily identified much later, after the pods have formed. Small, dark brown, elongated circles form on leaves and pods. On the leaves, there may be purplish streaks in adjoining leaf veins. In wet weather when many spores are being produced, the spots may have pinkish centers. Older spots on pods reach the beans inside, resulting in dark brown or black spots on the beans. These resemble small open wounds, but they usually lack the wet appearance of the spots on leaves and pods. Seeds produced by bean plants that show evidence of anthracnose on leaves, stems, or pods should be regarded as contaminated, even if you can't see any dark spots on the seeds.

Melon and Cucumber. A slightly different species of anthracnose fungus causes problems on several cucurbit crops, especially watermelon, cucumber, muskmelon, and gourd. Watermelon and gourd are most susceptible, though there is one anthracnose race that can devastate cucumber. All races of cucurbit anthracnose are most common in warm climates where rainy weather coincides with temperatures of 70° to 75°F (20° to 25°C).

The first symptoms of cucurbit anthracnose are dark brown to black spots on leaves. The youngest, most tender leaves are easy prey. Spots often begin on a leaf vein and may drop out in the center, leaving holes. Or, spots may become so numerous that the whole leaf shrivels and drops off.

By the time leaf spots become numerous, there are usually additional spots on stems. Stem spots are elongated with dark margins. In wet weather when many spores form, a pinkish jelly may show in the centers of the spots.

Spots then begin to form on fruits. These look like wet, sunken bruises, and may range from ¼ inch to 2 inches (0.5–5 cm) across. As the fungus matures, the edges of these spots darken, and the centers show gooey pink collections of spores. At this point additional microorganisms may grasp the opportunity to move in and cause the blemished fruits to rot quickly.

Anthracnose-infected cucumbers taste bitter, and infected watermelons lack sugar and flavor. Any seed developed inside infected cucurbits will probably carry anthracnose fungus inside the seed coat.

Rose, Grape, and Bramble Fruits. These plants may fall prey to anthracnose in warm, humid weather. When this disease strikes, you will see small dark spots forming on the tops of leaves. The outer edges of the spots are usually darker than the centers. The spots are ragged in shape, and after a time the centers drop out, leaving holes. In grapes it is sometimes called "bird's-eye," since the spots have dark margins and lighter centers.

This form of anthracnose is inhibited by hot, dry weather, while prolonged periods of rain give it a big boost.

Immediate Action: With bean and cucurbit anthracnose, your best defense is to always use disease-free seed. Seed grown in the arid West is best, and that's what most seed companies sell. You can save your own seed if you see no evidence of this disease on your plants, but be very watchful when the right weather conditions occur for this disease.

If you diagnose the disease in progress, wait for dry weather and take out the infected plants. Anthracnose fungi need wet conditions to spread. As long as the leaves of nearby plants are dry, they will not "catch" anthracnose as you gather up diseased plants.

Many varieties of watermelon that are resistant to anthracnose are of very high quality. If you live in the Southeast where cucurbit anthracnose often affects watermelon, by all means choose a resistant variety. A few resistant varieties of cucumber also are available.

With grapes, berries, and roses, you may be able to nip anthracnose in the bud by pinching off spotted leaves as soon as you see them. Even if the spots are caused by a disease other than anthracnose, this measure will slow its spread.

However, pinching off leaves is no match for a week of very wet weather. If you suspect anthracnose is present and warm, wet weather just won't let up, you may be able to stop the spread of the disease by using one of three organic fungicides: sulfur, lime-sulfur, or bordeaux mix (a copper/sulfur/lime concoction). These fungicides can penetrate leaves and kill living fungi and spores, but they also can damage leaves if they are not applied correctly. Follow package directions exactly when using these products, and pay close attention to the weather. Ideally, you should apply them early in the morning on a sunny day. These fungicides are poisonous to people and to beneficial insects. Wear protective clothing (long pants, long-sleeved shirt) to avoid getting them on your skin. If using a dust, wear a mask to avoid breathing the dust. Change clothes and bathe or shower when you are finished handling these fungicides.

In addition, practice good garden sanitation. Clean up and dispose of all leaves that fall during the summer and in fall. Also, replace mulches used on plants that show evidence of anthracnose. The next summer, if problems become worse, consider getting rid of the diseased plants and starting over in a new place with vigorous new stock. Many varieties of grape, blackberry, and raspberry offer good resistance to anthracnose.

Future Management: The increasing availability of disease-free seed and resistant varieties has made anthracnose much easier to manage. Still, gardeners in regions where the weather seems to bring out the worst in this disease should be always on the lookout for early symptoms. Since anthracnose has a weak talent for overwintering, there is always good reason to hope that next season will be free of this disease.

Apple Scab, Pear Scab

Type of Organism: A fungus, probably imported from Europe, classified as *Venturia inaequalis*. A closely related species, *Venturia pyrina*, causes scab on pears.

Host Plants: Apple and pear.

Where It Occurs: Apple scab occurs wherever apples are grown except the Coastal South (where few apples are grown). It is relatively mild in semiarid climates. The fungus that causes pear scab is also widely distributed and most common in cool, humid climates.

Making a Diagnosis: Apple scab is the most common disease of apples. It infects both leaves and fruits, though few gardeners notice the small bumps on leaves that develop in late spring. Commercial growers, however, are quite aware of the life cycle of this fungus. In damp years, many orchardists spray fungicides more than a dozen times in an attempt to keep apple scab from ruining the beauty of their crop.

Continuous spraying is not practical for home gardeners, who can manage apple scab differently with only a few dwarf trees to maintain. The first step is understanding how this disease operates.

Apple scab begins its yearly cycle in spring, when spores are released from infected leaves that fell the year before. Near neglected trees, these spores blow freely on the wind. Whenever temperatures are above 45°F (7°C) and leaves are wet, the spores may land on apple (or pear) leaves and establish themselves within hours. Unlike some fungi, apple scab fungi don't immediately penetrate deep into the leaf and cause dark leaf spots. Instead, they remain close to the leaf surface. The only evidence that they are there are drab, barely noticeable olive green spots, about ¼ inch in diameter.

The leaf spots release spores, some of which may land on green fruits and establish new fungal colonies. If many of the fruits that fall naturally in late spring show brownish spots near the blossom end and are not shaped quite right, a bad scab year may be in progress. When scab infects young green apples or pears, it robs the fruits' skins of their elastic properties and causes them to lose their symmetrical shapes.

When temperatures rise beyond the mid-80s (30°C) in summer, apple scab fungi take a break and stop spreading. Then, in late summer when temperatures cool down, the fungi again become active. Fruits that have almost reached mature size are then infected, often near the blossom (bottom) end. The blossom end dries out last in wet weather.

As the fungal patches mature, the skins of these fruits show light corky spots that are quite unsightly, but only skin-deep. Unless the spots are so large and numerous that they cause the fruits to split, the apples (or pears) are edible, though not pretty enough to sell.

Meanwhile, this fungus makes its final hurrah by developing a last round of infection on tired leaves. As these leaves fall to the ground, the fungus finally penetrates them and enters its resting phase, where it remains through winter. Then, when warm spring rains tell the fungus the time is right, millions of spores burst out of the dead leaves, beginning a new round of apple scab.

Immediate Action: For home gardeners, the most practical way to man- age apple scab is to maintain a high level of sanitation around apple trees. Get rid of elderly, neglected trees on your property. When choosing new varieties, look for apples adapted to your area that show some tolerance of scab. Your Extension agent can recommend the best choices.

When fruits fall in late spring, or when you thin them back by hand, gather up every one that hits the ground and either compost or bury them. Sometimes scabby leaves shrivel and fall early as the tree tries to clean itself. Gather these up as well and place in a hot compost pile (see page 14).

The most important tactic is to rake up leaves that fall at the end of the summer. Compost them in a pile that heats up to 130°F (54°C). If left in place, these leaves will be the primary source of next year's infection.

Future Management: You will never get rid of apple scab permanently, because you can't control the weather or the spores that blow in on the wind. However, the combination of excellent sanitation and resistant varieties can give you heavy harvests of fruits with only a little scab here and there.

Bean Rust

Type of Organism: A fungus named *Uromyces phaseoli* var. *typica* causes this common, widespread disease. More than thirty slightly different races of the fungus have been identified.

Host Plants: Beans, especially bush snap, pole, and dry beans. Many varieties are tolerant, but none are highly resistant. Scarlet runner bean and lima bean rarely get this disease.

Where It Occurs: Bean rust is distributed worldwide, but since the fungus requires mild temperatures (around 70°F, 20°C), coupled with high humidity, it's not often seen in dry, arid climates.

Making a Diagnosis: The first thing to watch is the weather. For rust to develop, bean leaves must stay damp continuously for several hours, and predominantly damp weather must persist for three to five days. Temperatures between 68° and 72°F (20°–22°C) favor the development of rust.

The first signs of rust are small, white, blisterlike spots on leaf undersides. Within days these spots turn an orange-brown color, hence the name of this disease. Spots are usually circular in shape. As the disease progresses, leaves turn brown and drop off. The fungus gradually infiltrates all the cells on leaf undersides. In advanced cases, stems and pods develop rust spots as well.

By the time the spots on the first affected plants turn orange, the disease will have spread to neighboring plants. Spores usually are produced within a week after the disease episode begins and may be spread by wind, water droplets, or the gardener moving among plants. Insects, tools, and stakes also may be responsible for spreading rust spores.

Immediate Action: Since leaves must remain damp for the rust fungus to flourish, thinning crowded plants to encourage rapid drying of leaves is a good idea wherever rust problems have been known to occur. Thin when the plants are completely dry.

In a small garden, you can pick off affected leaves and dispose of them outside the garden, in a hot compost pile, if you manage to catch the outbreak in its early stages. If the weather seems to be working against you, and mild rainy weather persists, this measure may not have much impact. Instead, you may need to sacrifice the planting by pulling it up and composting it outside the garden.

If you have multiple plantings of beans, be very careful not to walk among clean rows after you have been working with infected plants. Rust spores easily become airborne, and can cling to shoes, clothes, and tools and are particularly easy to spread when leaves are damp.

Never turn under rust-infected beans, for the fungus can persist in rotting plant material for a year or more. If there is time left in the growing season, make a new planting of a tolerant variety in another section of the garden where beans have not been grown for two years.

If you consider your rust outbreak to be an emergency, you can spray your beans with sulfur or lime-sulfur, which will halt the spread of the fungus. However, these natural fungicides may harm beneficial insects and can burn plant leaves unless they are applied exactly according to package directions on a cloudy day.

A Few Related Rusts

A few Uromyces fungi occasionally appear on other garden plants, including pea, onion, corn, rose, shrubs, hollyhock and other flowers, and bramble fruits. Each strain of rust infects specific plants. In other words, bean rust can't infect corn, and rose rust can't infect beans. All rusts cause orange powdery spots on leaf undersides.

▲ *On peas, rust is rare and appears only occasionally rather than year after year. Rotate the planting site, use clean trellis material, and keep plants widely spaced to prevent future problems.*

▲ *Onions and asparagus may turn yellow and fall over from the same strain of rust. Rotate onions, and clean up winter debris of both crops to limit the fungus's opportunities for growth.*

▲ *On corn, rust may appear if corn is grown in the same soil or in adjoining plots for several years. Keep plants widely spaced, and grow resistant varieties where corn rust is present.*

▲ *On roses, rust is a Western United States problem. Pick off affected leaves and dust remaining foliage with sulfur to stop its spread.*

▲ *On brambles, rust is difficult to get rid of since it can persist in canes and stems from year to year. If the disease is severe, try mowing down all canes in early spring. You sacrifice the current year's crop, but may save the planting. However, if rust appears on the new growth in late summer, it's best to dig up and destroy the plants, and start a new bramble patch in a new place.*

See also white rust, caused by a different type of fungus, on page 83.

As a follow-up treatment for pole beans bothered by rust, disinfect poles and trellises at the end of the season by wetting them well with diluted bleach or other household disinfectant. Rust has been known to overwinter on bean poles.

Future Management: Since weather plays such an important role in the proliferation of rust, and beans are such valued plants in any home garden, you may need to be quite vigilant to prevent recurring problems with this disease. If you have seen rust in the past two years, grow only tolerant varieties and rotate beans so they grow in the same soil only once every three years. These actions, combined with adequate spacing, should keep you from having rust in all but the worst weather years.

Bush beans tend to be more rust tolerant than pole beans. Plus, since bush beans mature quickly, there is less time for rust problems to develop. Yet pole beans have better flavor, generally speaking, and also produce better for an extended period of time. Rust problems are usually most prevalent late in the season. Therefore, growing pole beans in spring and removing them from the garden in late summer can be an important aid in long-term control of this disease.

Black Rot of Cabbage

Type of Organism: A bacterium called *Xanthomonas campestris* causes this disease. Black rot is sometimes called bacterial blight or stump rot.

Host Plants: All members of the cabbage family, including cabbage, cauliflower, broccoli, brussels sprouts, kale, collards, mustard, radish, rutabaga, and turnip. Black rot of sweetpotato is a different disease; see page 65 for information.

Where It Occurs: Usually in pockets scattered in the northern half of North America. Yet this disease can be carried on seed and therefore may occur anywhere that contaminated seed is grown and weather conditions are warm and moist.

Making a Diagnosis: Black rot manifests a cluster of symptoms that makes it easy to identify. In order of appearance, they are:

1. Brownish yellow patches appear on leaves, usually close to leaf margins. Outer leaves that have been bruised by rain or wind usually show spots first, since the bacteria enter the plants through tiny breaks in the leaves. The patches are usually V-shaped, and are bordered by leaf veins.

2. Patches become more numerous, and whole leaves begin to turn yellow (between brown patches), shrivel, and die. Leaf veins darken. Meanwhile, growth may continue on the other side of the plant, creating a one-sided look. New leaves that manage to grow are smaller than they should be.

3. If you cut a stem crosswise, you see a dark ring inside, which indicates that the bacteria have thoroughly invaded the plant's vascular system. Depending on the plant affected, how old it is, and the seriousness of the infection, a sticky yellow liquid may ooze from the cut stem.

Black rot of cabbage is identifiable by the brownish yellow patches that appear on leaves.

Immediate Action: Since plants affected by black rot will never be pretty or productive, remove them from the garden at the earliest possible time. Delaying can contribute to the persistence of the disease in future years, and can cause your garden to stink. Although black rot doesn't smell bad by itself, the other microorganisms that move in to finish off diseased plants cause the classic stench of rotting cabbage.

Black rot bacteria do not live in soil for long periods of time; they must be on or near host plant tissue to survive. However, since most cabbage family crops rot slowly when turned under, the bacteria find ample host tissue unless all traces of previous cabbage crops are removed after harvest. It is therefore doubly important to rotate space used for crucifers (members of the cabbage family) where black rot has been seen.

It's also a good idea to pull up infected plants, keeping the root ball intact, and dispose of them far away from the vegetable garden.

For example, you might compost them at the opposite end of your yard, and use the compost on fruits or shrubs. Some old books recommend burning infected plants, but I know of no safe ways to get juicy broccoli or cabbage stumps to burn.

If the diseased plants were grown from seed of questionable integrity, get rid of any leftover seed. Never save seed from plants affected with black rot or from plants that grew near diseased plants.

Future Management: With a little forethought, you can virtually eliminate the chance that you will ever see black rot again. First, grow your own seedlings using a sterilized potting mix and certified disease-free seed. The safest seed is grown in the West, where black rot is very rare.

If you know nothing about the origin of your seed, or if it was given to you by another gardener, soak it in hot (120°F, 50°C) water for twenty minutes. This treatment kills black rot bacteria.

When possible, choose varieties known to be resistant. Some varieties of cabbage are much more resistant than others, and the same goes for broccoli. Remember that even resistant varieties of cabbage family crops should be rotated with beans, peas, or grains to safeguard the overall health of the soil and reduce the risk of black rot and other diseases.

Black Rot of Grape

Type of Organism: The fungus known as *Guignarida bidwellii* causes this widespread disease. There are at least two common subspecies.

Host Plants: American grapes and European/American hybrid bunch grapes. Black rot is seldom serious on muscadines, though a subspecies of the fungus does attack them. Tolerance to black rot varies greatly with cultivar.

Where It Occurs: Many areas east of the Rocky Mountains, especially where humid conditions prevail.

Making a Diagnosis: Leaves, flowers, fruits, and stems are infected by this fungus. In late spring after leaves have unfurled, they become speckled with irregular reddish brown spots that gradually darken. Infected flower clusters may wither without setting fruit. Later, when grapes are the size of peas, you may see small pale spots that become brown and eventually encompass the entire berry. Half of the berries in a bunch may shrivel into black, dried-up mummies.

The fungus is in its active reproductive mode whenever spots are visible on leaves or fruit. The fungus also may hide in the tissues on stems, though stems show no evidence of infection. Spores released by both leaf and fruit spots may blow for long distances on the wind. The disease is encouraged by damp weather.

Immediate Action: When black rot first appears, you may be able to save the plants by pruning off all affected leaves and removing and destroying infected fruit clusters. At the end of the season, rake up all fallen leaves and compost them in a hot compost pile. Never allow mummified berries to hang on the vines through winter, or to lie on the ground, for these mummies are a primary source of infection for the next year. Prune your grapes aggressively to further reduce the fungus's opportunity to establish itself.

If you grow several varieties of grapes, you'll quickly learn which ones are the most susceptible. Remove varieties that are chronically afflicted with black rot, and replace them with more tolerant varieties.

Future Management: Since home gardeners usually keep only small collections of grapes, this disease often can be managed by growing tolerant varieties and practicing excellent sanitation. Commercial growers follow a very intensive fungicidal spray program to control black rot, but gardeners may achieve equally effective control by watching their plants very closely and intervening at the first sign of trouble.

Before making an investment in grapes, check with your Extension agent for varietal recommendations. Grapes that are well suited to your climate and soil, and that show tolerance to black rot, are by far the best choices. Resistant or tolerant varieties are available within all classes of grapes, including American hybrids (Catawba, Concord), French hybrids (Chancellor), European grapes (Riesling), and muscadines (Thomas, Noble). Many newer varieties are tolerant, based on breeding work involving the above cultivars.

Black Rot of Sweetpotato

Type of Organism: A fungus named *Endoconidiophora fimbriata* causes this disease.

Host Plants: Sweetpotato and wild morning glory.

Where It Occurs: Primarily in warm climates where sweetpotatoes are often grown, but the fungus can be transported to new locations on diseased tubers, sprouts, and containers.

Making a Diagnosis: Sweetpotatoes infected with black rot are most often encountered in storage. Soft circular spots turn dark and become corky. In advanced cases, a black fuzz may cover the affected area. If eaten, the potato will taste bitter.

Sometimes tubers appear sound yet still carry the fungus. When these potatoes are used to grow slips (sprouts for planting), the slips carry the disease. Slips affected with black rot grow poorly, with leaves often appearing a sickly yellow color. The portions of the stem below ground may have small black spots on them.

Immediate Action: Slips or mature potatoes infected with this fungus should immediately be discarded. If left to grow, the fungus can become established in the soil, where it can persist for two to three years. Wild morning glory and other weeds serve as alternate host plants.

When handling diseased plants or potatoes, thoroughly wash tools with warm water to keep from spreading the fungus to other parts of the garden. When you discover black rot in stored potatoes, get rid of the boxes or other containers because they, too, can become contaminated with this fungus.

Commercial growers of sweetpotato slips routinely disinfect mother potatoes before bedding them. In place of the agricultural chemicals farmers use, gardeners can pretreat sweetpotatoes by soaking them in solution of 1 tablespoon (15 ml) borax per gallon (4 liters) of warm water for 20 minutes.

Whether you buy your sweetpotato slips or grow your own, snip off the bottom ½ inch of each slip just before planting. This is the portion of the slip most likely to be infected with black rot fungi.

During the growing season, black rot can be spread by nematodes, sweetpotato weevils, and other insects. Grow insect-resistant cultivars to limit this mode of transmission.

Future Management: Buy sweetpotato slips that have been certified disease-free if you have ever seen sweetpotato black rot on your homegrown crops. Rotate sweetpotatoes with other crops, and keep down surrounding weeds (especially morning glory) even when soil is not infested. These steps, combined with clipping off the base of slips, can drastically cut the risk of this disease developing. In addition, curing sweetpotatoes immediately after harvest by keeping them in a warm (85°F, 30°C), humid place for two weeks helps them to develop sound skins that seal out possible entry by this and other diseases.

Blackleg

Type of Organism: A fungus named *Phoma lingam*. It is also called Phoma wilt, foot rot, and canker.

Host Plants: All members of the cabbage family (see page 162), plus the flowers sweet alyssum and stock.

Where It Occurs: Most common east of the Rockies, under damp conditions. However, the disease can travel long distances on contaminated seed.

Making a Diagnosis: Unlike black rot, blackleg causes plants to wilt rather than turn yellow and then brown. The wilted leaves remain attached to the plants. Sometimes leaves turn purplish as they wilt. Small brown or gray spots appear on all plant parts. Later, black dots develop within the spots.

Wilting of the top parts of the plant can be traced to a growing sore, or soft canker, which develops on the main stem near the soil line. At first this may appear to be a broad, sickly bruise in the main stem. The roots of affected plants rot as well. As the canker becomes larger, the plant may fall over as the stem breaks.

Immediate Action: Pull up affected plants right away, because they stand no chance of recovering. Dispose of them in a hot compost heap far from the vegetable garden, and use that compost on shrubs or fruits.

The fungus that causes blackleg lives on tissue of host plants, which may take two full years to rot in some soils. Avoiding blackleg is another reason to rotate cabbage family crops with legumes, grains, and other unrelated vegetables.

Blackleg also can be carried on seed. Western-grown seed is usually free of blackleg, and most reputable suppliers of untreated seed sell seed that has been heat-treated to kill this fungus. To heat-treat questionable seed, soak it in hot water (120°F, 50°C) for 20 minutes.

Future Management: Some varieties are resistant to blackleg; use them if you have seen this disease in your garden. Where blackleg has not appeared, good garden practices combined with the use of clean seed keep blackleg from threatening plant health.

Brown Rot, Mummy Berry

Type of Organism: A fungus known as *Monilina fructicola* east of the Rockies. Its West Coast counterpart is M. *laxa*. A third species, M. *urnula*, causes mummy berry in blueberries.

Host Plants: Very common on peach, plum, and nectarine; also occurs on cherry, apricot, almond, and sometimes other fruits such as highbush blueberry (the types grown in cool climates).

Where It Occurs: Throughout the United States, but most damaging in the South and East.

Making a Diagnosis: As soon as peaches start to ripen, they suddenly develop a brownish rotting spot. By the next day, a fuzzy brown mold forms on the fruits. The same thing happens with other fruits. If you pick them when almost ripe and set them on a table in a warm room, brown rot usually develops within three days.

Should you leave the moldy fruits on the trees, they become mummies that remain attached to their limb through most of the winter. The fungus preserves the shrunken fruits so that when they finally fall to the ground they remain mummies until the following spring. Then, when temperatures rise and the trees flower, little mushroomlike appendages that look like tiny golf tees arise from the mummies. Spores burst forth. The powdery fuzz on the outside of fruits also become teeming masses of fungal spores.

Other symptoms include clusters of closely spaced blossoms that turn brown and rot. In severe cases, gummy sores or cankers develop on badly infected wood. This ooze also contains fungal spores.

Immediate Action: Commercial orchardists depend on sophisticated fungicidal spray schedules to keep brown rot at tolerable levels. In addition to the fungicides, insecticides are added after the fruits have set, since the wounds made in fruits by curculios and other insects often serve as entry points for the fungus. Should you want to go this route, consult your Extension agent for the suggested schedule. Don't be surprised if more than a dozen chemical applications are recommended.

But for most home gardeners, weekly spraying is neither practical nor desirable. Besides, if you have only a few trees to care for, you can make a great impact on brown rot by practicing excellent sanitation. Here's what you must do:

1. In winter, prune plants to shape them and to remove any wood that may host insects or disease. Dispose of the prunings outside the orchard. In late winter, before the buds swell, apply a dormant oil spray.

2. In spring, mow and rake beneath trees and apply a light, porous mulch of straw, weathered leaves, or shredded bark.

3. In early summer, clip off any clusters of blighted blossoms. Thin fruits to proper spacing so they're not crowded. Pick up and bury green fruits that drop to the ground by themselves.

4. As the fruits begin to ripen, pick promptly; avoid bruising. Remove moldy fruits from the trees and bury outside the orchard.

5. In fall, remove all mummified fruits you find, along with their attached stems. After the leaves fall, gather up all fallen leaves and twigs, and rake the area beneath trees clean. Gather up the tree debris and old mulch, and compost them outside the orchard. Top-dress trees lightly with compost. If desired, oversow lightly with clover or other hardy cover crop.

Future Management: Since brown rot spores blow freely on the wind, you can't completely eradicate this fungus from your yard. Still, the sanitation measures described above will enable you to harvest nice crops of peaches or plums, despite the prevalence of this disease. Some newer varieties offer improved tolerance of brown rot, but none are truly resistant. Blueberries usually develop problems only when they are seriously neglected.

If you intend to grow peaches, plums, cherries, or nectarines organically, brown rot is likely to be your biggest challenge. To improve your chances of success, do everything you can to grow strong, healthy trees. Choose the best adapted cultivars for your area, check the soil's pH at least once a year, fertilize at least once a year with rotted manure or another good fertilizer, prune trees every winter, and apply dormant oil sprays in late fall and in late winter to control insect pests. Keep a good fruit grower's handbook handy, such as Lewis Hill's *Fruits and Berries for the Home Garden* (Garden Way Publishing), so you will be able to find answers to questions that arise about how to best care for your trees.

Brown rot control sounds labor intensive, and it is. If you added up all the hours of work you do to control it, you might find you spend as much time meticulously maintaining your trees as you would following a fungicidal spray schedule. If you are just planting some trees, see if you can get the cultivars you want in a dwarf size. Trees that are small are easier to maintain than larger ones.

Double Blossom Rosette

Type of Organism: A fungus classified as *Cercosporella rubi*.

Host Plants: Blackberry, raspberry.

Where It Occurs: This disease has been seen as far north as New York but is most common in the Deep South.

Making a Diagnosis: The best time to see this fungus in action is in spring, when you can observe open berry blossoms. Flowers that look misshapen and mixed up, with little leafy protuberances in the flowers, may be infected with this fungus. Other symptoms include lots of petals, poor fruit set, and hard, grainy berries. The blossoms themselves may be clustered closely together.

Immediate Action: Nobody's quite sure what to do about this disease. It has become more serious as more people in the Southeast have started growing cultivated blackberry cultivars, almost all of which are susceptible to this disease. Since the fungus spreads when the blossoms are open, you can get good control by chopping down the plants before they flower. You won't get any berries that year, but you'll stop the disease cycle and will see little or no rosette for four or five years — the typical time required for this disease to establish itself in a berry planting.

Fungicidal sprays don't seem to do much to control rosette. Some people get good results by going through their berries at blossom time and cutting out every rosetted blossom they find. This reduces the load of spores that travels with the pollen and keeps the disease at tolerable limits.

Future Management: Until resistant varieties are developed, rosette will remain a threat to many blackberries and raspberries grown in the South. If you notice that a variety is especially susceptible to this disease, replace it with something else. It may also help to eliminate wild berries growing close to your cultivated ones, as wild berries probably host this disease, along with several viruses.

Downy Mildew

Type of Organism: This disease is caused by several different fungi that infect particular crops. On lettuce and many flowers the culprit is *Bremia lactucae*. The onion, cabbage, and spinach families suffer from several species of *Peronospora*, including the aptly named *P. destructor* species that infects onions. *Plasmopara* and close relatives infect carrots, grapes, and members of the cucumber family. The drawing below shows how similar these organisms look, hence their collective classification as downy mildew.

Host Plants: The list is extremely long and includes many flowers, all members of the cabbage family, all members of the cucurbit (cucumber) family, most leafy greens, and all onion relatives. Fortunately, downy mildew fungi are host specific, so the same species that infects lettuce can't live on cucumber. In most areas, a single form of downy mildew is much more common than others.

Where It Occurs: Downy mildews may occur wherever damp, cool weather prevails for more than a month. Most forms are not present in the arid West, since weather conditions there seldom suit the needs of this group of fungi. The ideal temperature range for most types of downy mildew is between 45° and 55°F (7°–13°C). Dampness — either from rainy weather, heavy fog, or crowded plants — is a necessary contributing factor. This disease is often more severe in the North than in the South.

Making a Diagnosis: Whenever you see plants that have yellow or light brown patches on the tops of leaves and a furry growth on the undersides, you're probably looking at downy mildew. Usually older leaves are affected first, especially those on the lower parts of the plant, which are the last leaves to dry off in wet weather. Once downy mildew is visible to the human eye, the fungus has reached its reproductive stage and is poised to spread rapidly.

Three Faces of Downy Mildew

Downy mildews survive primarily in plant tissues, though some produce special spores — the fungal equivalent of seeds — which may persist in soil for many years. Yet it would be misleading to call downy mildew a soilborne disease since it usually spreads on the wind, through splashes of rainwater, or on the bodies of insects. Note the fat little tips on the drawing below. Each of these is a new fungal organism that may find its way to unoccupied stomata on the same leaf or another nearby. Stomata are the "breathing holes" that exist all over leaves. Downy mildew fungi are masters at becoming parasites through the stomata on leaf undersides.

The long fruiting branches of all downy mildew fungi create the look and feel of soft down when they become numerous. The actual color of the down varies with the type of downy mildew in progress. The organisms hold themselves to leaves by inserting tubes into the stomata. As hard as you may try, you can never clean off downy mildew.

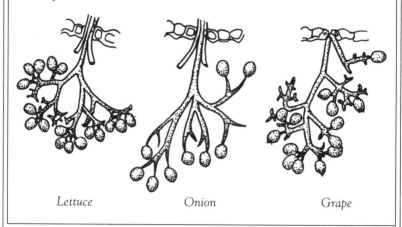

Lettuce   Onion   Grape

The specific color and pattern of the mildew on leaf undersides varies with the crop affected. On lettuce the mildew is a dingy yellow to brown, while on onion it's slightly purple. Spinach downy mildew is gray or light purple. On cucurbits, advanced cases of downy mildew may appear blackish, like a sooty mold.

In addition to exhibiting patches of mildew, seriously infected plants grow very slowly — if at all — or may shrivel and die. If they produce anything, much of the flavor will be lost. Cucumbers from infected plants are often tasteless.

Immediate Action: The first strategy for curbing downy mildew is to rotate crops, especially where the ground doesn't freeze much in the winter. Most downy mildews spend the winter in weed hosts and crop residue and are killed by freezing temperatures. Yet some produce spores (fungal "seeds") that can survive in soil for years. Whenever you've seen downy mildew on a crop, it's best to play it safe and avoid planting that crop in the same place for at least three years.

Another approach is to keep plants thinned to the spacing recommended for each crop on seed packets (or in gardening books). Sunshine is probably the greatest killer of the downy mildew fungus, which requires low light and high humidity to thrive. Carrots that are nicely thinned rarely contract downy mildew. Keeping plants widely spaced alters the environment to make it much less hospitable to downy mildew fungi.

If you catch downy mildew very early, pinching off affected leaves will slow the spread of the disease. This method can be quite effective if you have the cooperation of the weather. For example, if you clean up your spinach when only a few patches of mildew have appeared and several days of warm sunshine follow your pinching spree, the disease may go into remission. However, keep in mind that whenever you've seen a few patches of downy mildew on leaf undersides, thousands or millions of spores have already been released. If cloudy, wet weather continues, further damage is probably imminent.

Resistant varieties of many crops are widely available, though the reliability of that resistance varies quite a bit. Resistance in cucumbers is quite strong, and it so happens that the Oriental cucumbers plant breeders use to add downy mildew resistance to cucumbers also impart wonderful culinary characteristics. In melons, some varieties tolerate downy mildew much better than others, but none are truly resistant. In seed catalogs, the letters *DM* indicate downy mildew resistance. Good tolerance combined with warm, sunny weather substantially cuts the risk that melons will get this disease.

Vegetables that are normally grown when the weather is cool (temperatures conducive to downy mildew blowouts) have more serious problems with this disease. This situation is made worse by downy mildew's talent for adapting itself to changing food supplies. Resistance in a variety of lettuce or spinach one year may not hold up the next year. In Europe, downy mildew goes crazy on lettuce, and resistance must constantly be reestablished through breeding new varities. In the United States, spinach growers face constantly changing races. In a five-year period, three new races of spinach downy mildew were identified.

Finally, downy mildew can develop on cabbage and other crops after they have been placed in storage in a cool, humid root cellar, even if you didn't notice the mildew when the plants were in the garden. Check stored foods regularly for patches of downy mildew. Cut away all diseased portions, and preserve or consume affected foods as soon as possible.

Future Management: Because weather plays such an important role in the downy mildew life cycle, the odds are stacked against you if you live in a climate where cool, moist weather prevails for long periods of time. If you've seen the disease once, chances are good that you'll see it again. Take comfort in the fact that these fungi are obligated by their nature to attack only certain crops.

Fire Blight

Type of Organism: Bacterium indigenous to North America, classified as *Erwinia amylovora*.

Host Plants: Pear, apple, and all members of the rose family. Pears are the most susceptible of all, followed closely by apples.

Where It Occurs: The first identified outbreak of fire blight occurred in the Northeast 200 years ago. By 1910, the disease had spread throughout the country. Fire blight is considered epidemic in the Southeast and remains a formidable challenge in most areas where pears may be grown.

The results of fire blight, which is caused by a bacterium, resemble fire damage.

Making a Diagnosis: If you were to assault a pear or apple tree with a blowtorch, singeing tender green twigs back to where they join the stem, you would create a picture-perfect example of fire blight. This widespread and devastating disease of pears, apples, and many other plants is exactly what it claims to be: a blight that looks like damage caused by fire.

The leaves don't actually ignite. Rather, a very versatile bacterium invades the most succulent plant tissues and reproduces itself many times over. Under ideal conditions in late spring, it can double its numbers by dividing twice an hour. After a few days, the bacteria swarm out of the damaged cells. In early summer, when there are plenty of tender young leaves and stems to serve as habitat and temperatures rise into the 70° to 80°F (21°–27°C), fire blight bacteria are in their heyday. Adolescent and mature trees may suffer numerous blighted twigs during the first few summers of infection; younger trees may be blighted to death in only a year or two.

Fire blight bacteria can be spread long distances by flying insects, who inadvertently carry the pathogens on their bodies. In addition, fire blight bacteria are great swimmers. Whenever it rains, they float, swim, and splash to new locations within a tree, where they may get lucky and land on a spot that's ripe for colonization.

You can detect evidence of fire blight during the winter months or in late summer, when the bacteria are much less active. At the base of blighted stems, and on larger stems about ½ inch across, you'll see a darkened ridge that forms an irregular collar. This crater appears to have shrunk away from adjoining bark. It is the hiding place for resting fire blight bacteria and is often called a holdover canker. These cankers serve as reservoirs of infection. If left unpruned, the same canker can release eager bacteria for two seasons, or until the limb is dead.

In late spring little sticky droplets of ooze often weep from the cankers as the disease becomes active. This oozing gum is full of bacteria, ready to invade any cracks in bark or tender new growth it encounters.

Immediate Action: The first step is to grow only varieties that show some tolerance of fire blight. Your local Extension agent is the best source of information on pears and apples that meet the winter chilling requirements for your area and tolerate or resist fire blight. There are more resistant apple cultivars than resistant pears, for pears are more susceptible to fire blight by nature.

The next step is to prune thoughtfully and often. If you see young twigs blighting away in early summer, cut them off 4 inches below where the infection appears active. Soak your knife or pruning shears in a sterilizing solution of one part bleach to four parts water between pruning cuts to avoid spreading the bacteria. Burn the pruned twigs.

In winter, carefully inspect plants from top to bottom and prune off all limbs that show holdover cankers. If a branch has several cankers, prune off the entire branch. Gardeners who have only a few dwarf trees to maintain have no excuse for not spending a few hours every winter attending to this chore.

If fire blight is present but your trees are growing well, stop fertilizing in early spring. Spring fertilization is generally a good idea, since it gives new growth time to toughen before winter comes. However, trees that produce an overload of tender new growth in spring face an increased risk of fire blight, since they make such an excellent habitat for the disease. Instead of using fast-release chemical fertilizers in early spring, switch to slow-release organic fertilizers such as aged manure or blended vegetable meals.

Future Management: Good if you live where the disease is under reasonable control, select your trees carefully, and prune thoughtfully. In contrast, if you live in the Southeast, plant a susceptible pear, and then neglect it, it will eventually die. Before it dies, it will play an important role in spreading the disease to other people's orchards.

Halo Blight

Type of Organism: A bacterium variously classified as *Pseudomonas syringae* or *P. phaseolicola*.

Host Plants: Bean.

Where It Occurs: Long an established disease of beans in Europe, halo blight is seen most frequently in the eastern United States, rarely in the West. It moves to new places on contaminated seed.

Making a Diagnosis: This disease was epidemic in the mid-1960s, and now is much less common thanks to the increased production of disease-free seeds in the West and the use of resistant varieties. Still, halo blight can seriously threaten beans, especially when the bacteria infect young plants from contaminated seeds.

The best way to identify halo blight is by leaf spots. The bacteria enter leaves through wounds or stomata on leaves. There they colonize and cause small brown spots to develop. These spots are surrounded by light green halos, so it appears that each little brown spot lies in the center of a bleached-out area. The brown spots are usually smaller than those caused by other bean blights.

Weather plays a part in the symptoms of halo blight. The bacteria thrive in warm, damp weather. The halo is easiest to see when temperatures remain between 60° and 70°F (15°–21°C). At slightly higher temperatures, the halo is sometimes absent, but the spots grow larger.

The entire halo area around the spots turns brown and dies as the disease progresses. If the plants continue to grow, they do so slowly, and new growth is often dwarfed and crinkled. If the disease doesn't gain a foothold until blossoming is imminent, the plants may set some pods, but the beans will have no seeds in them, and the pods may show reddish brown speckles. By this time the bacteria will have spread throughout the plant, and some reddish brown streaks in stems may develop.

Immediate Action: As soon as you diagnose halo blight in your beans, pull up affected plants and deposit in a hot compost pile. If you don't, the bacteria may spread to every bean in your garden. Moving among wet bean foliage spreads this disease, as do violent thunderstorms that splash and blow the bacteria to new plants.

You should also assume that nearby beans have been exposed to the disease, even if they're not yet showing symptoms. Harvest them as soon as possible, and postpone plans to grow additional sowings of beans until next year.

Once halo blight has appeared in your garden, be very careful with your rotations. The disease can persist in dead plant tissue for perhaps a year, but to be on the safe side allow at least two years before you again plant beans where halo blight occurred.

Future Management: These days it's very rare to get contaminated bean seeds from reputable dealers. Still, it's a good idea to inspect any bean seeds closely before planting. Infected seed is often slightly shriveled with cream-colored spots. Never plant such seeds, or any others stored in the same container.

Several newer snap bean varieties are resistant to halo blight. If you live where this disease is especially bad, grow these resistant varieties.

Phomopsis Blight

Type of Organism: A fungus variously classified as *Phomopsis vexans* and *Diaporthe vexans*.

Host Plants: Eggplant.

Where It Occurs: Mainly in the Deep South and other semitropical areas, though the disease can travel widely on contaminated seed.

Making a Diagnosis: This fungus attacks all parts of the eggplant. On young plants, look for clearly defined brown spots on leaves, which gradually turn yellow and die. Young stems also can develop elongated circular spots that girdle the stem, causing the plant to die.

On fruits, the spots that develop as a result of phomopsis blight are usually quite large and show numerous concentric rings. This is a very ugly disease, capable of spreading rapidly from plant to plant in warm, wet weather.

Immediate Action: Pull up affected plants and chop them into a special compost heap. Use that compost only for fruits or ornamentals rather than returning it to the vegetable garden. In warm climates, this fungus easily survives winter living on dead and dying eggplant tissue. After the plants have been removed, treat the soil with compost to antagonize the phomopsis fungi.

Future Management: In areas where winters include numerous hard freezes, you may see this disease once, as a result of growing contaminated seeds or infected plants. However, it can't survive winter in cold soil and probably won't reappear in subsequent seasons.

In warm climates, especially Florida and similar latitudes, grow resistant varieties if you've seen phomopsis blight. Several are available. This disease infects only eggplant and is generally a small threat in home gardens. But just to be safe, rotate eggplant with legumes or grasses to keep this fungus suppressed.

Powdery Mildew

Type of Organism: Several closely related fungi. The ones most commonly seen by gardeners include *Erysiphe cichoracearum* on cucurbits and phlox, and *E. graminis* on grasses and grains.

Host Plants: Cucumber, squash, pumpkin, gourd, muskmelon, lettuce, pepper, potato, pea, bean, apple, cherry, grape, peach, strawberry, lawn grasses, cereal grains. Also numerous flowers including phlox, zinnia, dahlia, clematis, *Monarda*, salvia, and sunflower, plus some shrubs. Each plant family has a species or subspecies of powdery mildew unique to that group of plants. Cucumber and muskmelon can share the same strain of the fungus, but a slightly different form infects fruit trees.

Powdery mildew must overwinter in living hosts, which often include weeds closely related to cultivated plants. Trees and perennial plants carry the fungus from year to year in their buds or crowns. Once the fungus starts growing, it quickly spreads on the wind and on the bodies of insects.

Powdery Mildew Life Cycle

In early summer, warm temperatures and rainfall activate spores. When spores land on the leaf of an appropriate host plant, they quickly germinate and send a hypha — a "feeding tube" — into the outer cell. The bottom of the tube enlarges and anchors the fungus. This process takes only a few hours.

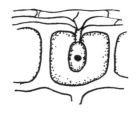

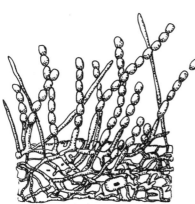

The fungus grows by developing branches (mycelia) over the invaded cells. Some of these rise in chains from the leaf surface, creating the powdery deposits. The powder consists of thousands of spores, which blow to new leaves and then germinate. Repeat "crops" of spores are produced every five to ten days.

In late summer the fungus changes its strategy. Production of summer spores gives way to winter spores, which are spore capsules with a protective outer coat. These are held in place by the fungi's branches. They wait through winter until spring weather causes them to burst open and spread to new leaves. The cycle then repeats itself.

Where It Occurs: Powdery mildew knows no geographical limits. It is mentioned in the Old Testament of the Bible and in ancient Greek writings. In the United States it occurs from coast to coast and, unlike many other fungal diseases, it lives quite comfortably in semiarid climates.

Making a Diagnosis: Leaves that look like they've been sprinkled with flour are unmistakable evidence of powdery mildew. Usually the powder is white, but it also can be dusty gray. Vegetables stricken with powdery mildew lose their vigor, and any fruits they manage to produce are tasteless.

In addition to showing a dusting of powder, leaves or buds may dry out, curl up, and die because the fungus dehydrates leaves. Powdery mildew fungi develop rootlike hyphae, that anchor themselves in leaves. These hyphae draw moisture from host plants, providing powdery mildews with moisture even in very dry weather.

Plants vary in how severely they suffer from powdery mildew. The severity of the disease also depends on climate. In areas where nights are cool and days are hot, powdery mildew runs rampant. Powdery mildew has the unusual talent of being able to establish itself on dry leaf surfaces. However, it must have a brief, two-hour period of high humidity to spread to a new leaf — a requirement easily met even in arid climates during the predawn hours.

Immediate Action: Powdery mildew is a formidable presence in many gardens. Since most forms can overwinter on nearby weeds, trees, or dormant buds, they can easily establish themselves as permanent residents in your yard and garden.

There are three options to consider: growing resistant varieties, treating with fungicides or fermented compost tea, or developing a tolerant attitude. Each of these has its place.

With vegetables, the best solution is to grow resistant varieties, especially in late summer when powdery mildew is at its worst. Resistant varieties of all of the most susceptible vegetables — cucumber, muskmelon, peas, and beans — are widely available. In seed catalogs, resistance is often abbreviated as *PM*. As an extra precaution, get to know several resistant varieties of each vegetable so you don't grow the same varieties year after year. Powdery mildew is known to mutate in order to invade a host plant that was previously resistant.

With fruits, the importance of resistance is even greater since, as perennials, they can host their own worst enemy from year to year.

Look for the most up-to-date varieties; mildew resistance in many fruits is a relatively new development.

When seed catalogs describe either fruit or flower varieties as "mildew resistant," they are talking about powdery mildew. Phlox and zinnia are highly susceptible, though some cultivars, such as Mexican zinnia, show good resistance. In addition to choosing resistant varieties whenever possible, place mildew-prone flowers where they will get copious sunshine. Low light favors the development of this disease.

The next step is to protect high-risk plants by dousing them periodically with strong sprays of water. Although gardeners are generally advised to avoid wetting plant leaves when watering to avoid spreading diseases, powdery mildew is a unique case. Recent research from England showed that strong rain (or turbulent sprays of water) can dislodge powdery mildew spores and slow the spread of the disease. When watering phlox or other plants that are likely to develop powdery mildew as the leaves age, do wash down the leaves by simulating a downpour.

Fermented compost tea also can inhibit powdery mildew (see page 38 for instructions on how to make it). Preliminary research from Germany indicates that when compost tea is applied to plant leaves before they are infected with powdery mildew, the tea is as effective as sulfur. In another study, compost tea applied to tomato leaves that were already infected did not eliminate the disease, but did slow its spread to new leaves.

In my own experiments, I have observed noticeable progress in controlling powdery mildew from applying compost tea every two weeks to plants that already show symptoms of powdery mildew. Plus, it's quite possible that the tea benefits plants nutritionally, since it does contain both major and minor nutrients.

However, there may be a practical problem here. It takes two weeks to ferment a batch of compost tea, and in that time a small powdery mildew problem may develop into a much larger one. While you are waiting for your tea to ferment, you may have luck using a baking soda spray to treat early outbreaks of powdery mildew on small fruits and flowers. Mix 1 teaspoon baking soda per quart of water; add ¼ teaspoon of mild soap to help the mixture stick. Repeat the application after one week. Between applications, give infected plants a thorough shower with water as described above.

Historically, sulfur sprays have been used to control powdery mildew on fruits, perennial flowers, and shrubs. If applied weekly, it can provide some control of powdery mildew and other fungal diseases. However, only use sulfur when temperatures are below 80°F (27°C) or you may burn leaves. Some mildew-prone crops can be burned by sulfur at lower temperatures, so check the label of the product you plan to use. Sulfur is also toxic to many beneficial insects. Wear protective clothing and a mask when applying.

Chemical fungicides are available that can control powdery mildew when properly used. If you decide to try one, read the label very carefully, because several well-known formulations are not effective against this particular disease. Usually weekly reapplications are necessary to keep the disease from reemerging.

A tolerant attitude comes in handy if you're not willing to give up growing susceptible plants and don't want to spend half the summer with a sprayer in your hands. Pick off the first powdery leaves you find and bury them at the bottom of your compost heap. With fast-growing annuals, make several sowings so you'll have healthy young replacements for older plants that contract this disease.

Future Management: Getting rid of powdery mildew once and for all is an impossible dream. Fortunately, we live in an age in which resistant plants are not hard to find and enjoyable to grow.

With perennial flowers, good exposure to sun and fresh air can reduce powdery mildew to a cosmetic nuisance. It may infect your phlox, lilac, or *Monarda* every year, yet the will plants continue to grow and prosper. Except in the case of young annuals, it's important to remember that powdery mildew causes stress, but seldom leads to death.

White Rust

Type of Organism: All white rusts are caused by various species of the *Albugo* genus of fungi. Specific species infect specific crops. The most threatening ones in gardens are white rust of spinach, *Albugo occidentalis*, and white rust of cabbage, *A. candida*.

Host Plants: Spinach, cabbage, beet, and their close relatives; sweetpotato; numerous flowers; and some herbs. Various forms of white rust usually appear as unexpected epidemics. They are quite rare in home gardens. In the case of flowers, the fungus can be imported on bedding plants.

Where It Occurs: All areas, with most outbreaks occurring in fall during periods of cool, wet weather.

Making a Diagnosis: White rust is easy to identify. No other disease causes yellowish to white blisters to form on leaf undersides, which then erupt into pebbly patches of chalky white powder. Blisters also may form on stems, but older leaves growing close to the ground are the most typical sites of infection. Above the white patches, the tops of leaves show yellowish spots.

White rust is an odd disease that must overcome substantial barriers to gain a foothold in a garden. Each strain can infect only its particular host plant. For example, white rust of cabbage can't infect spinach; white rust of turnip can't spread to sweetpotatoes. Within species of white rust are specific races; the races that infect cabbage and Chinese cabbage are slightly different.

White rust depends on plant tissue to survive from year to year. It lives on plant tissue that is not completely rotted; once the host plant has completely decayed, the fungus perishes. So, unless you grow a lot of a susceptible crop (or somehow import contaminated plants), you may never see this disease.

In addition to these hurdles, white rust requires cool, wet weather to prosper and spread. Like orange rust, the spores blow on the wind but must have a wet leaf surface in order to establish themselves. Some races that attack the cabbage family grow best when subjected to intermittent chilling.

To balance these challenges, the fungi that cause white rust are extremely talented at establishing themselves once they find a hospitable leaf. The organisms quickly multiply until they become so numerous that they burst through the leaf. The cottony white powder that erupts from leaf undersides contains clusters with thousands of spores.

Because of this complicated life history, white rust usually occurs in epidemics, when all its requirements — for host plants, inoculum, and weather — come together. By the time you see the white chalky eruptions, you can assume that an epidemic is well under way, at least for that particular species of plant.

Immediate Action: Immediately pull up infected plants and destroy or compost in a hot, active compost heap. Assume that all nearby plants of the same species have the disease, though blisters and white patches may not yet be evident. Harvest those plants.

Future Management: As long as an outbreak of white rust is stopped while in progress, the likelihood of seeing the disease in subsequent seasons is low. However, to be safe, rotate crops just in case some infected plant tissue remains in the soil. Legumes don't get white rust, so they're a good choice for planting in gardens where this disease has been seen.

◄ CHAPTER 4 ►

BLOTCHES, SPOTS, AND SPECKS
Leaf Spots and Other Foliar Diseases

Plant diseases that attack leaves are extremely common. Leaves are the most obvious places for fungal spores to alight, germinate, and thrive. Most leaf spots are the work of various fungi, though a few are caused by bacteria.

In order to develop into a disease, most of these microorganisms need a place to enter leaves, so the character of the leaf surface plays an important role in disease transmittal. For example, most members of the cabbage family have a waxy coating on their leaves that leaf-spot diseases can't easily penetrate. Plants with thinner leaves are much easier to invade, not only because they lack a protective coating, but because they're more likely to have minuscule wounds through which diseases can enter. When rain or hail pounds down on a leaf, it causes numerous bruises and small cuts that serve as access points for plant diseases. However, not all leaf-spot diseases require a wound. Some can enter leaves directly or through the stomata, "breathing" holes on the leaf surface.

The hairiness of plant leaves also affects their propensity to develop leaf-spot diseases. The numerous little hairs on the leaves of tomatoes and beans, for example, hold moisture on the leaf surface, and that moisture makes it easier for fungi to survive. This doesn't mean that hairy leaves are bad. Leaf hairs often are primary means of defense against tiny insects such as mites and aphids, which often become mired in the hairs as they try to feed. Since insect feeding often invites diseases, the fewer bugs you see, the better.

Leaf-spot diseases also are influenced by the curliness and texture of plant leaves. Tomatoes with curly leaves are very slow to dry out, which puts them at high risk for several leaf spots that crave wet conditions. In comparison, pepper leaves — being flat and not so hairy — are seldom bothered by leaf spots since they dry out quickly. Plants with brittle leaves often are easily injured because they break rather than bend when beaten by heavy rain or harsh winds.

Not all leaf problems are diseases. When clean, open holes suddenly appear in leaves, but you see no insects around, you may be looking at the work of night-flying beetles and moths. See Chapter 8 for descriptions of insect feeding patterns that resemble leaf-spot diseases.

Don't worry. A little bit of injury — whether from insects or leaf-spot diseases — actually can be good for plants. As long as the injured (or eaten) parts constitute less than a third of the plants' total leaf surface, the plants' productivity probably won't be affected. In fact, a bit of leaf chewing often triggers an alarm within the plant to quickly alter its leaf chemistry to be less appetizing to insects. With diseases, the plant may attempt to stop the progress of the disease by simply dropping the leaf.

Frequently leaf-spot diseases move beyond leaves and also cause spots on plant stems. The outer cells on plant stems often are quite similar to those on leaf surfaces and share many of the same functions. The stems on green-stemmed plants carry on photosynthesis just as the leaves do, which explains why nearly leafless plants like the Novella variety of garden pea produce well despite their lack of leaves. When a tomato is stripped of most of its leaves by early blight, it continues to grow a bit since the stems can take over some of the physiological work usually done by leaves.

COMPOST TEA THERAPY

One innovative method that can be of special use against many leaf spots (and other fungal diseases) is the application of fermented compost tea, described in detail on page 38. This amber elixir contains a banquet of assorted microorganisms that may impair the success of the ones that cause leaf spots and other diseases.

The effectiveness of compost tea, while not fully understood, can probably be explained three different ways. First, the sudden arrival of many fungi and bacteria on plant leaves may trigger the plants' own self-defense capabilities. Second, the new microorganisms, particularly bacteria, inhibit the growth of fungi; or third, the new ones may simply win out in the natural competition for space and nutrients.

Before applying the tea, clip off expendable diseased plant parts — a task best done when the plants' leaves are dry. In early evening or on a cloudy day when there is little threat of burning plant leaves with spray, apply the tea liberally to both sides of plant leaves until the whole plant is dripping wet. Use a watering can if you have a lot of plants to cover. Repeat every two to three weeks.

USING OTHER FUNGICIDES

Commercial fungicides can be used to fight leaf-spot fungi, but they must be used regularly or they won't do any good. Except for systemic fungicides, which are synthetic (not organic), fungicides work by forming a film over plant leaves that fungi can't tolerate. If rain washes off the fungicide, your protection is gone.

There are naturally derived fungicides that can be especially valuable in controlling diseases of tree fruits. Sprays made of sulfur, lime-sulfur, or copper often give excellent control of some of the less persistent fungi that bother fruits. Bordeaux is a mixture of all three, available at most garden supply stores. Perhaps the best example of a responsive case is the fungus that causes peach leaf curl, which usually can be eliminated with a single properly timed application of one of these products.

Do be careful when working with these natural fungicides, for they can burn some plant leaves. Use them only on plants that are listed on the label, and follow label directions exactly. Otherwise, you may accidentally injure the plants you sought to protect.

The following mini-encyclopedia of ten common leaf-spot diseases is arranged in alphabetical order by common name. Some diseases discussed in other chapters also cause spots to develop on plant leaves. For help in making a correct diagnosis, see Chapter 9, pages 158–181.

COMMON LEAF-SPOT DISEASES

Alternaria Blight, Early Blight, Purple Blotch of Onions

Type of Organism: Various *Alternaria* fungi, including *Alternaria solani* on potato and tomato, and *Alternaria dauci* on carrot. On carrots, Alternaria blight is often called late blight. Yet another Alternaria on onion is called purple blotch.

Host Plants: Potato, tomato, carrot, onion, and an assortment of wild plants.

Where They Occur: Mostly in the Northeast, mid-Atlantic, and South, though wind and contaminated seed or plants can cause outbreaks in any humid climate. Seldom seen in arid places.

Making a Diagnosis: Early blight is one of the most common diseases tomatoes are likely to get. Although potatoes do get it, the fungus usually doesn't become well established on potato leaves until late in the season, and by then the potatoes are often ready to dig. The fungus can spread from potatoes to tomatoes. The fact that potatoes usually are planted a month to six weeks ahead of tomatoes in the spring sets the stage for crossover infection, since tomatoes become most susceptible just after they have set fruit, or at about the same time the fungus starts flourishing in the potato patch.

In both potatoes and tomatoes, Alternaria, or early blight, causes similar spots on leaves. These gradually become so numerous and widespread that the leaves wither to brown (usually without first turning yellow) and then hang from the stems. The dark blackish brown spots usually start out more or less circular in shape and occur first on the lowest, oldest leaves. With a hand-held magnifying glass, you can see concentric rings that make the spots look like a topographical map of a body of water. Eventually the centers become somewhat scabby with lighter brown margins. As the disease worsens, the spots become less circular and may run together. The sections of leaf just beyond the spots often turn yellow.

When leaves are infected, stems usually have smaller black spots that aren't as scabby looking as the ones on the leaves. As the fungi mature and become numerous, they may release toxins that destroy leaf tissues between the spots, leading to total browning and withering of leaves. Toward the end of the disease cycle, the edges of doomed leaves turn blackish brown.

The fungus that causes the disease produces spores which rise in chains from the leaf surface, though you would need a microscope to see them. Wind, rain, and insects spread the spores, which enter leaves easily through any injured surface, including abrasions caused by blowing sand or heavy rain. Warm, humid weather encourages the fungus, which multiplies fastest when temperatures are about 85°F (30°C) and there is plenty of slightly aged leaf material around to infect.

On carrots, Alternaria blight often begins as dark brown to black spots on older leaves. The spots elongate into streaks, which also appear on stems. When the disease is severe, most of the carrot foliage falls down into a brown mat, leaving only a tuft of new leaves erect. The plants are seriously weakened and may loose flavor and texture.

On onions, leaf spots begin as small bruised spots that quickly turn brown. They become larger very fast, eventually forming streaks 1 to 2 inches long down the leaves. As they grow, they temporarily take on a purple hue that fades to brown. Diseased leaves fall over. As the disease spreads, a large stand of plants can be weakened seriously.

Immediate Action: In a home garden, there are several ways to minimize losses from early blight on potatoes and tomatoes. The first is to grow potatoes that mature quickly, so you can get them harvested before they become seriously diseased. Never plant potatoes right next to tomatoes, for fungal spores can easily spread from one crop to another. Collect potato plants after you get the tubers, and compost the stems and leaves to make them rot quickly.

With tomatoes, look for varieties with flat, uncurled leaves; those with brittle, curly leaves are more likely to contract early blight. Grow your own seedlings from certified disease-free seeds, or buy plants guaranteed to be healthy. Plant tomatoes where neither potatoes nor tomatoes were grown the year before.

When the first spots appear on leaves in early summer (usually lower down and toward the inside), try clipping them off. This will slow down the growth of the fungus, but won't prevent it entirely. Some spores probably are present on stems, and you can't clip stems off without removing good green tomatoes.

After you see the first leaf spots and you know blight is developing, try spraying plants with compost tea (see recipe on page 38). Compost tea contains numerous assorted fungi that may outcompete the Alternarias for the basic necessities of life, slowing the growth of the blight fungi. For this approach to have maximum impact, keep splashing on the compost tea every two to three weeks.

These strategies help, but by far the most effective method for managing early blight (which often occurs late in the season) is succession cropping. Old leaves get this disease very easily, but young leaves on plants that have not yet set fruit rarely become infected, even when they are constantly bombarded with spores from older plants in the garden. Set out some plants early, but leave space for more plants to be set out in early and midsummer. By delaying planting of some of your tomatoes, you should have a good chance of seeing less blight on the plants set out last.

With carrots, the fungus that causes this disease spreads very rapidly, especially in wet weather. If the carrots are of mature size, go ahead and dig them up. Do not attempt in-ground storage of carrots suffering from blight. Several newer varieties of carrot are resistant to this disease.

Purple blotch of onions may largely be prevented by rotating crops, as the disease usually starts in contaminated onion tissue from the previous year. However, spores may be blown in on the wind. If leaves are bruised or weakened by other diseases or insects, *Alternaria* fungi can become established very quickly.

Future Management: *Alternaria* fungi can live on tomato seeds, and any composter knows how easily these survive from year to year in compost and soil. It's therefore highly unlikely that you'll ever get rid of early blight — it's a fact of life in many areas. Still, careful rotation of potatoes, tomatoes, and carrots with other vegetables that are resistant or immune to Alternaria fungi can go a long way toward reducing future problems to an occasional nuisance.

If you always see early blight on your tomatoes, start keeping track of varieties that have the fewest leaf spots. Tolerance varies greatly with variety. And, although no varieties are currently listed as resistant, a few may show impressive tolerance in your garden.

Several scientists are working to develop varieties that are resistant to early blight. Already, a few tomato varieties have an A after their variety name, which stands for Alternaria. Unfortunately, this resistance is to a minor disease called Alternaria stem canker, which is different from (and not nearly as widespread and serious) as the Alternaria fungus that causes early blight.

Angular Leaf Spot

Type of Organism: A bacterium classified as *Pseudomonas syringae*.

Host Plants: All members of the cucumber family, especially cucumber, muskmelon, and summer squash. Rare on winter squash and watermelon.

Where It Occurs: May develop wherever cucurbits (members of cucumber family) are grown, and can be carried on contaminated seed.

Making a Diagnosis: Leaves develop small angular spots that turn brown, often along leaf veins. The dead tissue becomes crisp and falls out, leaving small ragged holes in leaves. Spots also may develop on fruits, though this seldom occurs in home gardens. The worst problems with this disease develop where cucumbers or muskmelons are grown repeatedly, for the bacteria overwinter in host plant tissue in the soil. If the bacteria is given a chance to establish itself in the soil and in mature seeds dropped by infected plants, an outbreak becomes much more likely.

Immediate Action: Harvest fruits promptly, then pull up the plants and chop them into a hot compost heap. Do not grow cucurbits in that soil again for at least two years.

Future Management: Very good, for this disease can be conquered through crop rotation. In addition, many modern varieties of cucumber offer genetic resistance to angular leaf spot.

Black Spot

Type of Organism: A fungus named *Diplocarpon rosae*.

Host Plants: Roses of all types. Yellow hybrid teas often are the first infected. Some cultivars are more tolerant of black spot than others, though all roses, including shrub types and old-time antique roses, can develop this disease.

Where It Occurs: In all areas where roses are grown. It is most severe in humid climates, as wet leaves are needed for the fungus to spread. The disease easily travels from place to place on plants that may host the fungus on their canes.

Making a Diagnosis: A true leaf-spot disease, black spot is the most common speckler of roses aside from insects. The first spots usually develop on the upper sides of older leaves on the bottom half of the plant. They differ from other leaf spots because black spot lesions have spidery, fringed edges. If you look closely with a magnifying glass, you may be able to see the fine branches of the fungus forming the spots. After a couple of weeks, the centers of the spots may have black dots or pimples in them.

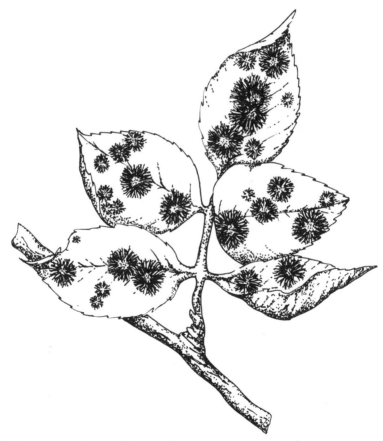

Black spot, prevalent in all areas where roses are grown, is the most common speckler of roses aside from insects.

Under favorable conditions, spots may suddenly become very numerous, so that some leaves have up to a dozen spots. At this point the leaves are so stressed that they begin to turn yellow, first around the margins of the spots. Gradually the leaves wither and drop off. After a few weeks, the plants will try to grow new leaves. These, too, will develop spots if the disease is out of control.

Immediate Action: It's important to wait until the leaves are completely dry to do anything about black spot. If you move among infected roses while the leaves are wet, you can easily spread the spores. The spores need wet leaf surfaces to attach themselves to the leaves.

Many people who grow show-quality hybrid tea roses depend on an intensive, weekly fungicide spray schedule to keep black spot at bay. However, the average gardener who grows only a few roses for their blossoms and fragrance usually can manage the disease without resorting to fungicides, except perhaps for sulfur. If you decide to follow the fungicide route, keep in mind that effectiveness will hinge on regular applications. A single shot will not do much good.

If you see only a few leaves with black spot, promptly pinch them off and dispose of them far away from your roses. Follow up with a drench of fermented compost tea (see page 38 for directions for making this fungus-fighting brew).

Keep clean mulch around your roses, and replace it each spring with new material. Since black spot is often spread by heavy rains splashing the fungus from leaf to leaf, a mulch slows black spot down by reducing the amount splashing.

Trim roses often to remove spent blossoms and canes that are causing the bush to be crowded. When fresh air and sunshine can penetrate the plants easily, the leaves will dry out faster, making it harder for black spot to gain a foothold.

If black spot is present, use drip irrigation or another watering approach that keeps water off the leaves and close to the ground. Remember, a primary strategy for fighting this disease is to keep leaves as dry as possible. Avoid watering late in the day, when leaves tend to dry slowly.

If one plant seems to develop black spot every year while others do not, get rid of that plant. It probably will have chronic problems forever, and will serve as a source of infection for your other roses.

Future Management: Choose tolerant cultivars whenever possible, but don't expect to see the word *resistant* used to describe any rose's reaction to black spot. Observe your plants closely and keep track of each cultivar's tolerance to this disease. Three years after planting three varieties that were supposed to be highly tolerant, I found that one of the three consistently developed spots, while the other two did not.

Avoid grouping yellow roses together, for they are often the most susceptible. Yet there are exceptions to every rule. A friend has a robust grandiflora yellow rose that develops hardly any black spot at all, though other plants nearby are covered with it.

At winter's end, prune roses hard to remove all leaves left from the previous year. Since the fungus can persist from year to year on canes, be especially aggressive when pruning plants that showed signs of the disease the previous summer.

Finally, inspect your roses often so you will catch black spot in its early stages. Pick up fallen leaves that may host the fungus. It's virtually impossible to get rid of black spot where the disease has firmly established itself, but close monitoring can keep it seriously suppressed.

Cercospora Leaf Spot   *sir-kos´-per-uh*

Type of Organism: Several species of fungus of the *Cercospora* genus. Specialized species infect particular crops.

Host Plants: Peanut, soybean, southern pea, beet, carrot, and many weeds.

Where It Occurs: Primarily in warm, humid climates and places where peanuts, soybeans, and beets are widely grown.

Making a Diagnosis: Cercospora is often called "frog-eye" leaf spot. The spots are usually circular, somewhat raised, and may have a yellowish halo around each so that they resemble a frog's eye. They first appear on the oldest leaves, and in times of warm, humid weather quickly spread to other plants. Frequently, as the disease becomes advanced in beans or peanuts, dead leaves begin to litter the ground around affected plants. Leaves die when spots become so numerous that they cover entire leaves.

On beets, spots are brown or brownish gray with reddish purple margins. The *Cercospora* species that infects carrots usually spots the youngest leaves first and gradually spreads to older ones. Both leaves and stems show circular light gray or tan spots with darker margins.

Immediate Action: Since this fungus can be spread by contaminated seeds, the first step is to plant seeds that are certified disease-free. If you saved your own seeds and see spots on the leaves of very young plants, chances are good that the seed was contaminated.

Another preventive measure is to rotate crops. Cercospora fungi live in dead plant material, so if you plant southern peas where infected peas were grown the year before, the chance of infection is very high.

In situations where you see the disease for the first time, try picking off the first spotted leaves to halt the progress of the disease. Then, get the crop out of the garden at the earliest possible time. Cercospora spores enter leaves through the stomata and germinate very quickly. The longer infected plants stay in the garden, the greater the chance that the disease will spread and persist. The disease also can be spread if you move among infected plants while the leaves are wet. The spores require wet leaves in order to germinate and grow. Mild, wet weather encourages this disease. It is usually most severe in fall.

Future Management: In a home garden, you can prevent Cercospora leaf spot by using the above methods and growing resistant varieties. Keep plants well thinned to promote the rapid drying of leaves after rain. Stay out of the garden when leaves are wet.

Of equal importance is cleaning up diseased plant debris and getting it out of the garden quickly. Compost these plants and leaves, and use the compost on flowers or ornamentals rather than in the vegetable garden. A little cercospora will not ruin a garden. It seldom kills plants outright but does weaken them and reduces yields.

Gray Leaf Spot

Type of Organism: A fungus classified as *Stemphylium solani*.

Host Plants: Tomato, pepper, eggplant, occasionally potato.

Where It Occurs: Mostly in warm, humid climates.

Making a Diagnosis: The leaf spots caused by this disease are similar to those caused by septoria leaf spot (see page 102). However, with gray leaf spot the spots tend to be flatter, somewhat gray in color, quite irregular in shape, and the centers of the spots often drop out. So, by the time the disease eats up a leaf, it will show little holes where the spots were instead of a whole, shriveled leaf. When young plants are infected, followed by warm, damp weather that promotes the spread of the fungus, all the leaves may eventually die except the newest leaves near the growing tips.

Immediate Action: Try the same measures that have some impact on other leaf-spot diseases of tomato: Pick off affected leaves promptly, keep leaves as dry as possible, and drench with fermented compost tea every two to three weeks. In warm climates, prune back tomatoes after they bear heavily in summer, both to reduce drought stress and to shortcut leaf-spot diseases like this one. The new growth that appears in fall may show little evidence of gray leaf spot.

Future Management: Since warm, humid weather promotes the growth of this fungus, it may be a recurrent visitor every year in many sections of the South. The fungus overwinters in dead plant tissue, so be careful to rotate tomatoes. At the end of the season, pull up plants and compost them instead of turning them under. If you use tomato cages, remove all vines and foliage from the cages in fall rather than waiting until spring. If you don't, some fungal spores may be waiting for your new plants as soon as you enclose them in contaminated cages.

Late Blight

Type of Organism: A fungus, *Phytophthora infestans*.

Host Plants: Potato and tomato.

Where It Occurs: This disease is widespread in the the Southeast and also occurs in the mid-Atlantic and Northeast during warm, damp seasons. The windborne spores can travel thirty miles or more, so the disease often spreads northward during the summer.

Making a Diagnosis: Late blight is quite different from early blight, but not because one disease comes early while the other comes late.

Especially in the Southeast, late blight can occur quite early in the summer. However, in northern areas it's not customarily seen until late July or August. The ideal conditions for late blight are temperatures between 60° and 70°F (15°–21°C), with 100 percent relative humidity for fifteen hours or more.

Late blight develops on both potatoes and tomatoes. It's not unusual for the fungus to become established on potatoes and then move on to tomatoes. Yet you don't have to grow both crops to see late blight. Windblown spores can infect either crop.

To identify this disease, look for rather large, medium brown to black spots on leaves. Older leaves that grow close to the ground (and therefore stay wet longer) are usually the first to go. Frequently the spots are bordered by one of the central leaf veins. During periods of damp weather with temperatures just below 70°F (21°C), the spots may expand quite rapidly. Plants can be nearly destroyed in only three days.

Late blight leaf spots do not have the concentric rings characteristic of early blight. With late blight, the edges of the splotches may be a little darker than the centers but will not have rings. The spots caused by late blight also are larger, with less clearly defined margins, than the spots caused by septoria leaf spot (page 102) or gray leaf spot (page 96).

If mild, wet weather continues, you may see another symptom on the undersides of affected leaves. Below the brown spots, leaf undersides appear gray and dead, and may show a margin of white cottony sprinkles. If the spots on the tops of the leaves look like late blight but you're not sure about the undersides, pick a few spotted leaves and place them in a plastic bag with a damp paper towel. Keep the bag at room temperature. Twenty-four hours later you should be able to see the white spore masses on leaf undersides, especially with the help of a magnifying glass.

In a garden, leaves spotted with late blight are releasing spores, even if you can't see the white deposits under the leaves. Because the disease likes mild weather, it will sometimes start on potatoes, subside, and then show up in late summer on tomatoes, after temperatures have cooled and fall rains have begun.

In very advanced cases, late blight can cause potato tubers to develop a reddish brown dry rot that extends from the skin into the tuber. Tomato fruits also can rot from this disease. Tomato fruit rot caused by late blight appears on green fruits as grayish areas, often on the sides or shoulders of fruits, which become brown and wrinkled. If potato tubers or tomato fruits show these symptoms, there will also be a large number of blighted leaves, with additional light brown patches on stems.

Immediate Action: To intervene, pick off any suspicious leaves and dispose of them in a hot compost heap. The fungus can live from year to year in seed potatoes but dies when exposed to cold winter temperatures.

After blighted leaves have been removed, douse plants with a baking soda solution made from 1 teaspoon baking soda per quart of water, with a few drops of mild soap added to help it stick. Cover both sides of leaves. After a week, check plants again and repeat the process if needed.

If late blight has not appeared in your garden but you've heard it's present in your area, begin a preventive program. Thin potatoes if they are crowded, and begin applying fermented compost tea every two weeks (see page {38}). Douse your tomato plants too. Prune tomato plants if growth is so rank that fresh air and sunshine cannot reach all of the leaves in the top halves of the plants.

This disease needs wet conditions to spread, so keeping leaves dry can help quite a bit. Late blight can be very serious on either crop, especially if it gets an early start on potatoes. Don't plant both crops in adjacent rows. When late blight gets out of control, it saps the energy from plants, causes them to lose many of their leaves, and ultimately reduces the quality and quantity of your crop.

Future Management: Since you can't stop summer thunderstorms from rumbling up from the South, you can't stop late blight spores from entering your garden. If you live where late blight is common, consider buying your seed potatoes instead of planting potatoes you grew yourself. If you buy certified disease-free spuds, you can rest assured that they won't carry late blight.

Genetic resistance is not available in tomatoes, though vigorous cherry tomatoes often show more tolerance than varieties that develop large fruits. Some potatoes do show resistance to late blight. If you live in a high risk area and plan to grow a lot of potatoes, seek out the highest level of resistance you can find.

In much of the Southeast, you can count on seeing late blight on tomatoes, even if you don't grow potatoes. Dousing the plants with compost tea at least once a month can discourage late blight and other leaf spot diseases.

Where the growing season is long, start a second crop of late tomatoes from seed in early summer rather than propagating cuttings from the plants you set out in the spring. This way, you will know that your late plants will not have blight before you even set them in the garden. Never plant tomatoes after potatoes in the same growing season.

Northern Corn Leaf Blight/Southern Corn Leaf Blight

Type of Organism: Two related fungi cause these diseases. The northern version is *Helminthosporium turcicum;* its southern counterpart is *H. maydis.*

Host Plants: Corn and other grains and grasses.

Where They Occurs: Southern corn leaf blight may occur wherever corn is grown, particularly in the lower Midwest and South. Northern corn leaf blight develops primarily in the North Central states.

Making a Diagnosis: The leaf spots caused by southern corn leaf blight are tan, elongated areas, usually ¼-inch wide and less than 1-inch long. They usually develop when temperatures are warm (between 70° and 90°F, 21° and 32°C), and rain has been frequent. As the disease worsens, the spots run together until most of the leaves are tan.

Northern corn leaf blight causes much larger spots, which are often several inches long and ½-inch wide. They begin as gray-green areas and quickly change to tan. The best temperatures for northern corn leaf blight range between 65° and 75°F (18°–24°C).

Both of these leaf blights usually begin on older leaves that are closest to the ground. The fungus overwinters on undecomposed corn residue. As the leaf spots grow, they release many spores that blow on the wind to new places. Fortunately for gardeners, most sweet corn is tolerant to both diseases, though the combination of wet weather and the presence of a heavy load of spores can cause it to develop leaf spots.

Immediate Action: Keep your fingers crossed that the weather turns dry, for these fungi require wet conditions to spread. If your corn

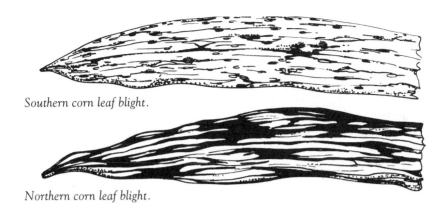

Southern corn leaf blight.

Northern corn leaf blight.

makes a crop, harvest it promptly and then turn under the stalks, or gather them up and compost them. Recultivate in fall to speed decomposition of the stalks.

Future Management: Epidemics of these diseases in recent years sent corn breeders scrambling to come up with resistant varieties. Since both diseases occur in multiple races, this was a huge task. Today, sweet corn varieties that tolerate both diseases are readily available. In seed catalogs, resistance to northern corn leaf blight is usually abbreviated as *NCLB*; southern corn leaf blight is *SCLB*. If you live in the Corn Belt where spores from a neighbor's field easily blow into your garden, make use of these resistant varieties. In other areas, choose resistant varieties if you can't rotate corn with other crops because of space limitations. Never leave diseased plants sitting in the ground longer than necessary, because the longer they stay there, the greater the opportunity for these fungi to thrive.

Peach Leaf Curl

Type of Organism: A fungus, *Taphrina deformans*, indigenous to North America.

Where It Occurs: May develop wherever peaches are grown.

Host Plants: Peach, nectarine, almond.

Making a Diagnosis: When peaches are infected with this fungus, leaves pucker and curl, became thickened and white to pinkish in color, and may drop off the tree in early summer. The fungus also may cause misshapen and cracked green fruits. If left uncontrolled, the leaf loss from this disease can seriously weaken trees and leave them open to other problems that can cause early death.

Immediate Action: You are most likely to see this disease if you inherit peach trees that have been neglected for a long time. There is little you can do during the summer months, as this fungus is inactive in warm weather. However, at the end of the season, raking up all fallen leaves is the first step toward promoting the tree's recovery.

The most important measure is to prune trees in late winter to remove limbs that are injured or unbalanced. Then spray a single application of lime-sulfur or bordeaux mix — two common, naturally derived fungicides. The ideal time to apply these sprays is late winter, just before the buds swell. However, any fungicide application made during the winter will likely control peach leaf curl.

Future Management: Excellent, since most gardeners are willing to spend a few minutes in winter treating this problem to ensure overall tree health.

Septoria Leaf Spot, Celery Late Blight

Type of Organism: A fungus known as *Septoria lycopersici* infects tomato. Other *Septoria* species sometimes cause leaf spots of currant and gooseberry, usually late in the season. *S. apii* infects celery.

Host Plants: Tomato, celery, currant, and gooseberry.

Where It Occurs: May develop on tomatoes in any area, but it's rare in the Northwest. The strain that affects celery is usually limited to areas where celery is grown on a large scale.

Making a Diagnosis: Since tomatoes have so many leaf-spot diseases, it's easy to get them confused. Septoria leaf spot is quite common. Often it is mistaken for early or late blights. Sometimes a single plant can show telltale evidence of all three diseases.

Septoria is primarily a disease seen from midsummer onward. On tomato, the spots are usually quite small, often ⅛ inch in diameter, and sprinkled over the leaves. At first, the spots are brown with darker margins and most evident on the top sides of leaves. The areas between spots turn yellow. Eventually badly affected leaves shrivel and die. Septoria spots develop on both new and old growth.

On celery, the spots start out yellow and are visible on both sides of the leaves. They then become gray and the leaves die. Gray streaks also appear in stems. The celery strain of *Septoria* is very contagious, as each leaf spot releases thousands of spores. It often strikes late in the season, and is commonly called celery late blight.

Immediate Action: Pinch off affected leaves and dispose of them in the compost heap. If the whole plant shows widely distributed septoria spots, begin spraying with fermented compost tea every three weeks. Don't let the small size of the spots fool you into thinking this disease is a minor nuisance. Even though the spots are small and the spores downright tiny, each spot may release five to ten thousand spores that are easily spread by wind, rain, insects, and gardeners. Their only weakness is that they need damp leaf surfaces in order to attach themselves and form new spots.

Future Management: Genetic resistance is not generally available in tomatoes, but you can plan your plot to minimize damage. Grow early determinates for canning and freezing, for these types of tomatoes usually are harvested before septoria gains a foothold. Pull up these plants after harvest to keep them from harboring septoria fungi. Meanwhile, keep midseason and late tomatoes well spaced and well staked to promote good air circulation among the leaves. Like many other spot-causing fungi, septoria thrive when leaf surfaces are wet.

On tomato, septoria leaf spot is more tolerable than other blights since it takes this disease a long time to seriously weaken plants, and it does not cause rot spots to develop on fruits.

With celery, small garden plots need careful crop rotations so celery is not grown in the same soil two years in a row. Never move among celery when the leaves are wet, for this disease is very easily spread because of the sheer number of available spores.

◀ CHAPTER 5 ▶

DEADLY CONSPIRACIES
Insect-Vectored Bacterial Diseases

Coming up against either an insect or a disease is a challenge for any gardener. When you encounter a situation where an insect carries, protects, and transmits a disease organism, you have a double challenge. Fortunately, such alliances between insects and diseases are rare except in the case of viruses, which are discussed in Chapter 6. Here we will look at three common bacterial diseases that are vectored by insects.

Many diseases can be carried from plant to plant on the bodies of insects, but these are chance events. Here we have insects that actually inject bacteria into plants as they feed. In addition to placing the bacteria exactly where they need to be in order to multiply (and multiply and multiply), the insect vectors benefit their charges by hosting them through many long winter days and nights. Without this winter protection, the bacteria might perish. Extremely cold winters may kill many of the insect vectors, which will greatly reduce disease problems the following summer.

As for the welfare of the vectors whose guts and mouthparts are laced with bacteria, they remain as healthy as individuals who carry no bacteria and whose bite is therefore less lethal. If an insect vector picks up some of the bacteria from feeding on infected plants, its offspring are not necessarily infected — until they feed on a contaminated plant themselves.

The main thing to remember about these deadly conspiracies is that if you can control the insect, you also control the disease. These bacterial diseases are not treatable once they enter the plants' vascular systems. Control efforts therefore must be directed toward the vectors. They may include choosing cultivars or varieties that are of little interest to the insect vectors, or keeping the insects away from the plants with floating row covers. Controlling these particular insects with pesticides — either natural or synthetic — is very difficult since the insects are so small and mobile. Plus, one bite is all it takes to infect a plant. Where insect and disease pressures are extremely severe, resistant varieties are your best option.

Bacterial Wilt of Cucumber

Type of Organism: A bacterium named *Erwinia tracheiphila*.

Host Plants: Cucumber, muskmelon, and occasionally pumpkin and squash.

Where It Occurs: Mostly in the central parts of the United States, with limited problems in the West, North, and South.

Vector: Striped and spotted cucumber beetles.

Making a Diagnosis: Bacterial wilt usually strikes cucumbers and muskmelons after they have developed vines. Sections of vine will suddenly begin to wilt and within a week will die. Remaining sections of the plant close to the crown may remain healthy for a while, but eventually they wilt, too.

There is also an ooze test you can conduct to confirm the presence of bacterial wilt. Cut an infected stem crosswise, and gently squeeze the stem while pressing your finger to the cut. Slowly pull your finger away. If a sticky white ooze forms a thin thread between your finger and the stem, this is evidence of bacterial wilt. Healthy stems emit no white ooze.

Bacterial wilt of cucumber often exibits a sticky white ooze when the cut skin is separated.

Immediate Action: No amount of watering or pinching back has any impact on bacterial wilt. The bacteria that cause the disease multiply invisibly in seemingly healthy plants. By the time symptoms become evident, the bacteria have become so numerous that they are choking the plants with their bodies and ooze. Frequently cucumber beetles infect plants while they are quite young, but it takes a few weeks for the plants to show signs of wilt.

Since infected plants can't recover, pull them out. This may reduce the numbers of the next generation of cucumber beetles that carry the disease.

A better approach is to prevent bacterial wilt by not allowing cucumber beetles near your plants. Because cucumber beetles can fly, insecticides are seldom successful in controlling them. Floating row covers, however, give excellent control and also protect plants from other insects.

With most varieties, you can cover the plants as soon as they are in the ground by laying a large sheet of floating row cover over them and weighing down the edges with boards. Some people bury the edges, though this is a messy operation. Whichever method you choose, use an oversized piece of row cover, and allow plenty of slack in the middle. Once cucurbits get growing, they expand really fast.

When the plants begin to flower well, you'll need to open the row covers to permit bees and other insects to pollinate the flowers. Don't rush to do this, because the first flowers may be all infertile males. Male flowers have only a bare stem at their base, while female flowers have a tiny green fruit between the stem and the blossom. Wait until a week after the first flowers appear to remove the row covers. By then, there should be a nice mix of both male and female flowers, ready to cross-pollinate and set fruit.

A few varieties of cucumber are self-fertile and can be grown under cover until the fruits are mature. Look for the word *parthenocarpic* in catalog descriptions to find these varieties. So-called greenhouse varieties also are self-fertile, but these must be grown on trellises under perfect conditions to produce well when grown outdoors.

No melons are parthenocarpic, so they always need their row covers lifted to permit pollination. If you want to leave the covers open for a time and then recover the plants, spray them well with water to chase away insects before putting the covers back on.

You'll find row covers easier to manage if you use them with compact bush varieties. Varieties that produce long, sprawling vines or those that prefer to run up a trellis are poor candidates for row-cover culture.

If row covers are not for you, you can also try trapping cucumber beetles. The chemical compound that attracts beetles to cucurbits is concentrated just beneath the rinds of muskmelons and many cucumbers. Set out a dish of these rinds on a piece of sticky paper. Or, poison the bait with insecticide and trap the beetles that way.

To repel cucumber beetles and other cucurbit pests, many gardeners grow radishes among their cucumbers. These radishes are not to eat. Let them grow and flower while mingling with your cucumber vines. Another method used in some climates is to grow calendulas, which actually seem to attract cucumber beetles. When the beetles gather on the calendula blossoms, swoop down on them with a butterfly net, and get rid of them by drowning them in a jar of hot soapy water.

Finally, a growing number of cucumber varieties described as nonbitter lack the chemical compound that cues cucumber beetles to feed. However, this lack of bitterness appears attractive to spider mites, so you have to choose which pest you'd rather battle. Where bacterial wilt is widespread, nonbitter cucumbers are the best choice.

Future Management: If you've seen bacterial wilt once, you'll see it again. Even if you use row covers for five years, and manage to get bacterial wilt out of the systems of your resident cucumber beetles, some new beetles may be blown in by a gusty thunderstorm. Then you're back to the beginning. You will need the whole grab bag of control strategies described above to manage this disease.

Pierce's Disease

Type of Organism: Long thought to be caused by a virus, Pierce's disease is now known to be the work of a *Rickettsia* bacterium.

Host Plants: Grape. This disease is also hosted by many flowers and grasses, which show no symptoms.

Where It Occurs: May occur wherever grapes are grown, but most devastating in the Coastal South, Florida, and parts of California.

Vector: Several species of sharpshooter leafhopper.

Making a Diagnosis: Where this disease is common, new plants remain healthy for only one year. By their second summer, leaves begin to turn brown, growing tips shrivel in late summer, and roots die back. New growth is slight or nonexistent. Infected plants die by the time they are five years old.

Immediate Action: Destroy infected plants. Do not attempt to grow susceptible grapes where this disease is common. Tolerance is rare in all grapes except wild ones; your Extension agent can advise you on the best grape varieties to try. Some new bunch grapes bred in Florida and a few muscadines offer some resistance.

Future Management: Some grapes show tolerance (but not strong resistance) to Pierce's disease. Check with your Extension agent for varieties recommended for your area. Genetic resistance is your best weapon against this disease, for leafhopper control is virtually impossible, even when the most toxic pesticides are used. Leafhoppers are small enough to blow in the wind, and they are usually widely scattered, too.

Stewart's Wilt, Bacterial Wilt of Corn

Type of Organism: A bacterium named *Erwinia stewartii* causes Stewart's wilt, also known as bacterial wilt of corn. The organism is sometimes listed as *Xanthomonas stewartii*.

Host Plants: Sweet corn.

Where It Occurs: Most prevalent in the central parts of the United States, where sweet corn is frequently grown. The disease overwinters in flea beetles or on seed. Following very cold winters, outbreaks are rare.

Vector: Flea beetles.

Making a Diagnosis: Early corn grown in rich soil is easy prey for this disease, since succulent young plants attract flea beetles. Flea beetle feeding almost always precedes the development of Stewart's wilt, though the disease can also be carried on seed.

Plants affected with Stewart's wilt usually bear the marks of flea beetles — skeletonized, ragged sections on leaves. The bacterium that causes the disease gradually becomes established throughout the plant and clogs up the vascular system. New leaves are small with pale cream-colored streaks, and plants never reach full size. The dwarf plants may tassel prematurely. When very young plants are infected, they may wilt to death.

If you cut the main stem crosswise, often you will see brown discolored areas near the center of the stem. As with other bacterial diseases that cause plants to wilt, this disease clogs up the plants' vascular system with toxic bacterial gunk.

Immediate Action: Sweet corn infected with Stewart's wilt cannot recover and will not produce well. Pull up diseased plants and compost them. Stewart's wilt rarely survives in soil but often survives winter in the bodies of flea beetles.

Future Management: Many resistant and tolerant varieties are available. When infected flea beetles feed on resistant sweet corn, the corn does not contract the disease. Since flea beetles feed mostly in the spring, resistance is most valuable with early crops.

If you have your heart set on growing a nonresistant variety and Stewart's wilt is common in your area, wait for a summer following a severe winter to grow it. Or, grow your pet variety late in hopes that it will escape feeding by flea beetles.

Flea beetles like many other plants better than corn. In a small garden, they may be lured away from corn if radishes, beets, chard, or arugula are available at the other end of the garden. Arugula in particular makes a good trap crop. This flavorful green tastes best when young. To use arugula to lure and trap flea beetles, let some continue to grow past the prime picking stage, and kill off the flea beetles that congregate on the plants with sabadilla dust.

◀ CHAPTER 6 ▶

THE TINIEST TERRORS
Viruses and their Vectors

The most minuscule life forms that cause plant diseases are viruses. Viruses are so small that they are measured in nanometers, or billionths of meters. Only when an electron microscope is used to magnify them more than two thousand times can viruses be seen.

Basically, viruses are tiny morsels of RNA protected by a coat of protein. Somehow, the RNA of plant viruses communicates with enzymes in plant cells and commands them to become virus nurseries. The cells become slaves to the virus, until the plants use so much energy serving the needs of the virus that they can't adequately take care of themselves. All kinds of crazy things happen. Plants may wilt and die, or crinkle up and discolor, or suddenly gush forth with a spray of strange, infertile blossoms. It all depends on the virus and what kinds of demands it makes on the plant.

Viruses are generally called by their common names, which usually include the name of the plant most commonly affected by that particular disease (for example, tobacco mosaic virus). However, the same virus may be capable of infecting many plants that don't belong to the same family for which it's named. A good example is cucumber mosaic virus, which can infect not only the cucumber family, but tomatoes, spinach, beans, and several common weeds.

No matter how sharp your eye or how well you think you know your plants, do not expect to always make the right guess when diagnosing viral diseases. Just as we refer to various runny nose syndromes as colds without knowing (or caring) what kind of virus is making us sick, it's perfectly acceptable to conclude that a plant has a virus without knowing which virus it is. Even scientists do this. Last summer, when a cluster of commercial tomato fields a few counties east of me was hit with a disease that caused the plants to wilt suddenly and die, the half-dozen experts who were called in concluded that the tomatoes had been hit with a virus, or maybe two or three. They did this by ruling out fungi and bacteria and piecing together telltale signs of viral infection.

Resistant varieties are available for some viruses in some crops, but not for everything. Breeding for viral resistance is slow work. Resistance that holds up in the lab may not hold up in the field. Plus, viruses are difficult to keep alive in the lab long enough to do something with them. Viruses can live only within plants or very specific insect vectors, with the exception of tobacco mosaic virus. If you have a box of virus-carrying thrips in the lab and they all die, there goes your experiment. And then there's the problem of mutation. If you're a virus, your whole being is a bit of RNA, so it's easy to change yourself.

Some viruses persist and occur year after year, yet the plants tolerate the infection well. In this case, the virus is barely a problem. At the other end of the extreme, viruses can occur in totally unexpected epidemics. These often come in cycles or may be very long lived. In the last twenty years, there have been epidemics of several viruses that lasted only two to three years. Scientists call these cyclical epidemics.

Here's how cyclical epidemics develop. First an aphid, leafhopper, whitefly, or other sap-sucking insect feeds on an infected plant, sipping up some virus particles in the process. Weedy host plants may be the beginning of the cycle. A week later, the infected insect has fed on a dozen plants (a conservative number) and spread the disease to each one.

Two weeks later, thousands of insect vectors have fed on these infected plants, picking up the virus in the process. At this point a very watchful gardener may see the first evidence of a viral disease. Windy weather then blows the insect vectors to a new location. They find suitable host plants, start feeding, and spread the disease. Meanwhile, new generations of vectors are feeding on more infected plants and moving in unexpected directions. Inside each infected plant, thousands of cell walls are bursting, releasing millions of new viral particles.

The Vocabulary of Viruses

Plant viruses have a special knack for interfering with a plant's production of chlorophyll in strange ways. Special terms are used to describe these antics, such as mottle, mosaic, streak, and stunt. Each word has special meaning when used to describe viral symptoms.

▲ **Mottle** describes a color pattern similar to paint-by-number pictures. On leaves, patches of yellow, light green, or tan are interspersed with dark green and the normal green color of the leaves. In pods and fruits, mottles often are somewhat circular and look like puddles of pale color beneath a waxy surface. Unlike leaf spots, the color patches of mottles lack defined edges.

▲ **Mosaic** symptoms usually involve mottling, with the additional complication of small leaf veins becoming involved in the trouble. As infected leaf veins take off in weird directions, the leaf becomes crinkled and stiff, like shattered glass. The failure of cells due to mottling and mosaic causes a shutdown of the delivery system that carries moisture and nutrients to the far edges of the leaf. Leaf edges curl upward or downward, or sometimes in both directions, and eventually wither and die.

▲ **Streak** looks like mottle, only it occurs in plants that have long, slender leaves like grains and grasses. Instead of pale circles or puddles of yellow, you see long streaks in leaves where chlorophyll's chores obviously aren't being done correctly.

▲ **Stunt** is often the clearest evidence that a virus is at work. Plants stunted by viruses continue to grow for a while, but the size of new leaves and the distance between them is dwarfed. Sometimes new growth looks like the plant has had a burst of energy, but instead of growing a new branch it develops a tuft of tightly packed, twisted foliage, or perhaps a spray of flowers that sticks up without its normal cover of leaves. Stunted plants have shortened internodes (the stem between new sets of leaves or branches).

Winter comes and goes, and some vectors survive and start the season by infecting plants. Or, the disease becomes so well established on host weeds that the cycle begins very early in spring and repeats itself with a vengeance. Finally a very cold winter comes, which kills overwintering vectors and/or host plants, so that the disease does not reappear until . . . the mystery wind blows in, and a new epidemic begins!

ABOUT VECTORS

Vectors are insects capable of transmitting diseases from one plant to another (the word *vector* in Latin means carrier). Bacterial diseases are sometimes spread by vectors, and viral diseases almost always involve a middleman.

Most vectors of plant viruses are very small insects themselves: aphids, leafhoppers, thrips, mites, and whiteflies. If you can control feeding by vectors, you can prevent viral diseases. But because the insects that act as vectors are small and usually quite mobile, they can be very difficult to eliminate. Floating row covers often provide some protection, but they must be kept over plants continuously. And some thrips have been known to find a way through these barriers.

Still, suppressing the numbers of vector insects in your garden is always a good idea. The best way to accomplish this in most home gardens is simply to invite the vectors' worst enemies to stick around. Lady beetles, predatory flies and tiny wasps, and many other beneficial insects are much better equipped to conquer little insects than are we humans.

Like all living creatures, beneficial insects need food and habitat to live happily ever after. For food you have your little insects to offer. Many beneficials are attracted by plants that produce a lot of pollen, like daisies, tansy, and corn. Perennial bushes or herbs can be important since they provide year round shelter for these helpful little beasts.

The following mini-encyclopedia of eighteen common plant viruses is arranged alphabetically by common name. To find out which disease may be bothering a certain plant, consult the table in Chapter 9.

COMMON PLANT VIRUSES

Aster Yellows

Type of Organism: Aster yellows is caused by an organism that is smaller than a bacteria yet larger than a virus, called a mycoplasma. Since the disease is transmitted among plants by leafhoppers, just like a virus, the general approach to understanding and dealing with it is the same as for true viruses. Another disease often referred to as yellows is Fusarium wilt (page 34), a fungal disease that lives in soil.

Host Plants: Aster, lettuce, carrot, celery, parsley, New Zealand spinach, and occasionally the cucurbit family, along with numerous flowers.

Where It Occurs: At least two strains of the organism that causes aster yellows are known. The western strain is common from Idaho to California, while the other strain occurs in widely distributed pockets throughout the rest of the country.

Vector: Primarily the six-spotted leafhopper.

Making a Diagnosis: When this disease strikes asters and other flowers, new growth looks yellow, stiff, and dwarfed in an odd way. New

Aster yellows causes carrots to loose their cylindrical shape, and new leaves to be small and yellowish.

growth appears with some enthusiasm, but it is abnormally stocky and brittle. Few if any flowers are produced.

On carrots, aster yellows causes new leaves to be small and yellowish, all growing tightly together. Older leaves often develop reddish coloring. Carrots lose their cylindrical shape and become bulging at the top and spindly at the bottom. Small feeder roots become curly and hairy. One look at a carrot stricken with aster yellows and you know something is desperately wrong.

Lettuce in which the heart leaves are small, crinkled, and sickly looking may have aster yellows. The stalks inside of infected celery plants are small, twisted, yellow, and may be cracked.

Immediate Action: To keep the disease from spreading, pull up and compost infected plants as soon as you find them. The disease cannot persist in decomposed plant tissue. Meanwhile, do what you can to control leafhoppers.

Future Management: Pretty good except on the West Coast, where this disease has a strong foothold. Some newer asters are yellows resistant, but they still may host this disease. To increase your chances of success with susceptible crops, grow them under floating row covers.

Bean Mosaic Virus

Host Plants: Bean (snap bean, dry bean).

Where It Occurs: Common bean mosaic was once a widespread disease but has largely been brought under control through use of resistant varieties and disease-free seed. However, new strains have emerged over the years, and there is always some lag between the time a new strain is seen and the time resistant varieties are tested and released.

Vectors: Many different species of aphids including bean, cotton, southern pea, cabbage, peach, and turnip aphids.

Making a Diagnosis: Regardless of the exact strain of the virus at work, mosaic on beans looks largely the same. New leaves are small, stiff, and yellow. Older leaves begin to show yellow mottling and curl under. New growing tips die. If the beans produce, pods are mottled with yellow, dark green, and brown.

Immediate Action: Pull up affected plants immediately and compost them. Encourage predatory lady beetles and other beneficials to keep aphids in check. For the remainder of the season, grow only resistant varieties.

Future Management: Excellent unless you are faced with a new, previously unknown strain of bean mosaic virus. Most of the leading snap and dry bean varieties are resistant to two strains of bean mosaic, though some older varieties are not even tolerant.

Cauliflower Mosaic Virus

Host Plants: Cauliflower, cabbage, broccoli, and closely related plants.

Where It Occurs: In isolated pockets throughout the country. Most common in warm climates.

Vector: Cabbage aphid and other aphids.

Making a Diagnosis: Most of the classic symptoms of viral infection are present with this disease. Leaf veins are light, leaf surfaces are mottled with yellow and dark green, and new leaves are small and curled. Plants are stunted, and production is low.

Immediate Action: Pull up affected plants and compost them.

Future Management: Cauliflower mosaic is rarely seen in home gardens but may occur once in a blue moon as a local epidemic.

Cucumber Mosaic Virus (CMV), Spinach Blight

Host Plants: Cucumber, squash, melon, and pumpkin are highly susceptible. Spinach, pepper, and tomato also may be affected. Special strains of cucumber mosaic sometimes infect celery, lima bean, and southern pea. Delphinium, lily, petunia, and other flowers may be affected. Many common weeds are host plants.

Where It Occurs: Widely distributed throughout North America. Usually develops as localized epidemics in warm climates.

Vectors: Several aphids, including cotton, lily, peach, and potato aphids. Cucumber mosaic also may be carried for short periods of time on seeds.

Making a Diagnosis: When cucumber mosaic infects members of the cucumber family, the leaf characteristics known as mosaic are clearly visible, usually just after the vines begin to run. Leaves become mottled with yellow and green, and the edges curl up and become brittle. New leaves are small, mottled, and crinkled. If squash fruits develop, they are heavily warted, misshapen, and too light in color.

Cucumbers fruits, if any, are watery, bitter, and mottled with yellow subsurface spots. Depending on the level of CMV tolerance of the variety being grown, the plants may decline slowly or rapidly.

On peppers the older leaves become mottled with brown, and fruits are mottled with yellowish-tan circles. If the variety being grown is tolerant to cucumber mosaic, a few affected leaves may fall off, but the plant may recover and bear sound peppers.

Tomatoes infected with cucumber mosaic virus show a set of symptoms known as shoestring. The edges of leaves virtually disappear, so all that's left are the leaf veins with a bit of tissue left near leaf tips. New growth is dwarfed and the whole plant is stunted. Production is minimal; fruits become mottled while still green and fail to ripen properly.

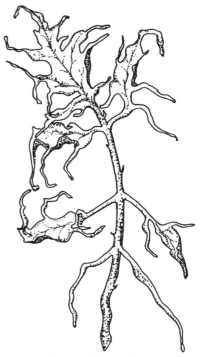

Tomato plants suffering from cucumber mosaic virus exibit "shoestring" symptoms as the edges of the leaves virtually disappear.

On spinach, cucumber mosaic virus is often called spinach blight. It occurs mostly in early summer, from spring-sown crops. New leaves are yellow and small, with a bleached out appearance. Older leaves become mottled and crinkled. Once this decline begins, it continues steadily.

Immediate Action: Pull up affected plants immediately to keep aphids from feeding on them and then passing the disease on to other plants. Chop them into a hot compost heap where they will decompose quickly. During the remainder of the summer and during the following year, grow only resistant varieties.

Future Management: Following an outbreak of cucumber mosaic virus, step up your weed control efforts, as this disease can overwinter in ground cherry, milkweed, ragweed, and other common weed species. Aphid populations often decline late in the season as natural predators become more numerous and active, resulting in a reduction in the prevalence of cucumber mosaic virus. Severe winter weather can radically reduce the number of aphids that survive to spread this and other viral diseases, interrupting cyclical epidemics.

Where cucumber mosaic virus has been seen, grow resistant varieties of cucumber, melon, and spinach. No squash varieties are truly resistant, but some are more tolerant than others.

With peppers and tomatoes, choose varieties that are resistant to other viruses, such as tobacco mosaic virus. These may show superior tolerance to cucumber mosaic virus.

Curly Top Virus (CTV)

Host Plants: Numerous plants, but most important on beet, bean, cucurbits, and tomato. Other plants are susceptible including petunia, nasturtium, and many other popular annual and perennial flowers.

Where It Occurs: Mostly in western areas where sugar beets are grown, but it can spread when infected leafhoppers are blown about or on plants shipped long distances.

Vector: Beet leafhoppers.

Making a Diagnosis: The name of this virus gives an important clue to its symptoms. New growth is small, twisted, and curled. With beets, the leaf veins become thick and lose color, and the roots develop thick mats of curly roots. On other plants, stems become stiff, short, and rigidly upright. Tomatoes show a pronounced yellowing of leaves, and this disease is often referred to as western yellow blight or tomato yellow. Wilting does not occur early on, distinguishing this disease from Fusarium wilt (see page 34). But the occasional twisting of a tomato leaf on otherwise healthy plants does not indicate curly top virus. More likely, it's a temporary "growing pain" caused by a starch imbalance during a period of rapid growth.

When plants of the cucumber family become infected with CTV, old leaves turn yellow yet new leaves are an unusually dark green color. Plants may continue to grow despite the disease, but they are weak and do not produce well.

Beans infected with curly top develop dense tufts of new leaves that gradually curl down at the edges. The leaves may be yellowish or very dark green, and the plants rush into flowering. Pods are few, sparsely filled, and small.

Immediate Action: Pull up and compost plants as soon as you see them to keep the disease from spreading. For the remainder of the season, plant only resistant varieties. Some gardeners find that beet leafhoppers stay away from plants that are shaded. In very hot areas where most plants appreciate shade, consider using shade covers to discourage the vector. Floating row covers also can provide temporary protection from beet leafhoppers.

Future Management: If you live where sugar beets are widely grown, or where the beet leafhopper is a common garden insect, consider your garden at high risk for curly top virus. Plant as early as possible, and check with your local Extension agent to find out when the beet leafhopper normally migrates to your area. This usually occurs when beet fields are harvested. The leafhoppers then migrate, often hundreds of miles, and many end up in home gardens.

If you can zero in on the time when beet leafhoppers are expected, cover susceptible crops with floating row covers to keep the vectors from feeding on them. Many varieties of squash and bean are resistant to curly top, but tomatoes are only moderately tolerant.

Lettuce Mosaic Virus

Host Plants: Mostly lettuce, but other leafy greens may become infected.

Where It Occurs: This virus has become established in most areas where lettuce is grown on a large scale. If there are lettuce fields within fifty miles, there is a chance you will see this disease in your garden. Lettuce mosaic virus also can be carried on seed.

Vector: Green peach aphid.

Making a Diagnosis: The symptoms are similar to cucumber mosaic virus. Leaves become mottled with yellow, developing a mosaic pattern of crinkling on leaves. In lettuce that forms heads or thick, stiff leaf ribs (including the French crisp or barrel-shaped heading varieties), there may be dark streaks in large leaf veins.

Immediate Action: Immediately pull up affected plants to keep the disease from spreading. Since home gardeners usually grow small plots of several different lettuces, you may find that one variety is affected while others are not. To protect healthy plants from disease-carrying aphids, spray them with water or a mild soap spray and then cover with a floating row cover.

In many areas where this disease is common, local ordinances require both growers and gardeners to grow seed that has been screened for the presence of lettuce mosaic viruses. In catalogs, this is usually noted by the letters *MTO* or *MI* (for mosaic indexed). Seeds that have been tested cost a little more, but as any gardener knows, a few lettuce seeds go a long way.

Future Management: Just because you start out with clean seed does not mean that your lettuce is resistant to this virus. Very few varieties are, and these are mostly romaines. And just because some plants show symptoms does not mean that all of them will succumb to lettuce mosaic. Take all the precautions you can, and grow varieties that mature quickly. Leafy lettuces (the types most gardeners prefer) often mature so fast that there is little time for mosaic to develop.

Maize Chlorotic Dwarf Virus, Corn Stunt (MCD)

Host Plants: All types of corn.

Where It Occurs: Mostly in the southern and central parts of the United States where Johnson grass grows wild in great profusion.

Vector: Leafhoppers. Johnson grass (*Sorghum halepense*), which is a persistent perennial weed, serves as a host for this disease during the winter months.

Making a Diagnosis: The word *chlorotic* describes plants that are unable to maintain their normal green color. When this disease strikes, corn leaves become tannish yellow, often with red streaks or margins. New leaves are the first to discolor.

In addition to changes in leaf color, corn plants are severely stunted when this virus is at work. A corn plant that normally grows to seven feet may attempt to tassel when it is only three feet tall. Any ears that are produced are small and contain very few kernels.

Immediate Action: Pull out and compost affected plants to keep the disease from spreading. Frequently this disease will infect some plants in a stand of corn, while others have no observable symptoms. Tolerance also varies with variety.

Future Management: In the unfortunate case that your property is surrounded by Johnson grass and this disease has become established, you may be in for a long, hard struggle. A few newer varieties of sweet corn are tolerant to this disease and to its sister saboteur, maize dwarf mosaic virus (below).

Maize Dwarf Mosaic Virus (MDM or MDMV)

Host Plants: Corn and other grasses.

Where It Occurs: Mostly in the central, eastern, and southern sections of the United States. This disease often develops in cyclical epidemics.

Vector: At least a dozen species of aphids.

Making a Diagnosis: Maize dwarf mosaic virus is more common than maize chlorotic dwarf virus (above), and its symptoms are a little different, too. Maize dwarf mosaic virus usually appears in early summer, when plants are 2 to 3 feet high and poised for rapid growth. But instead of growing up, they develop several tillers (suckers) and appear bushy. Leaves develop pale streaks in new leaves along with streaky mottling of yellow, dark green, and normal green. Dwarfing is very clear, as the main stem barely elongates so that new sets of leaves grow very close together. If ears develop, they may be tufted together in groups of two or three.

It's not unusual for virus-infected corn to show symptoms of both maize chlorotic dwarf virus and maize dwarf mosaic virus at the same time. Fortunately, corn breeders working on resistance to these diseases have found that varieties which are tolerant of one virus are usually tolerant to the other one as well.

Immediate Action: Pull up infected plants and compost them to stop the disease from spreading. Inspect corn weekly for evidence of this virus.

Future Management: Most of the aphids that spread this disease hit the air in midsummer, so early plantings usually escape serious damage. Even in epidemic seasons, early sweet corn is a safe bet.

In the next few years, several new sweet corn varieties that show good resistance to this virus should reach the market. Since some of the sweetest varieties are also the most susceptible, breeders have had a big challenge to create tender, sweet-tasting varieties that are also resistant.

Because this disease has multiple vectors and can overwinter on Johnson grass and a number of other perennial grasses, its potential for destruction is great. If your garden happens to be in the middle of an epidemic area, there may be very little you can do. Past epidemics have lasted two to three years. Future outbreaks should be less severe since many of the newer varieties of field corn offer some resistance. So, aphids that blow into your garden from nearby plantings of field or sweet corn are less likely to carry this devastating virus in coming years.

Pea Enation Virus

Host Plants: Peas (all types except southern pea), fava bean, soybean, clover.

Where It Occurs: Primarily in the Pacific Northwest.

Vector: Pea, potato, and peach aphids.

Making a Diagnosis: This very distinctive virus of pea begins with yellowish leaf spots that gradually turn white, especially on leaf undersides. The leaves also become crinkled, with small cracks and blisters evident on leaf undersides. Meanwhile, new growth is dwarfed and twisted, often turning sideways instead of growing straight up. Pods that manage to develop are small and twisted.

Immediate Action: Pull up affected plants and compost them.

Future Management: Very good if you plant only resistant varieties, which are now widely available. All peas with the Oregon State (OSU) initials attached to the variety name are resistant. Older varieties that mature slowly and grow tall, such as Alderman, are very susceptible.

Pea Mosaic Virus

Host Plants: Pea, fava bean, and clover.

Where It Occurs: Can occur anywhere, but most common in areas where peas are grown commercially.

Vectors: Pea, peach, and bean aphids.

Making a Diagnosis: This disease may not be a single virus, but one of several that cause similar symptoms on peas and fava beans. Leaves become crinkled and mottled with yellow. Leaf veins fade to light green, and new growth is lopsided and stunted. When more than one virus infects the same plant, leaves may become streaked with brown and gradually wither. Plants with slight symptoms, such as slight leaf mottling, may continue to bear.

Immediate Action: Pull up affected plants and compost them, unless the end of the pea season is right around the corner and the plants appear healthy enough to bear a crop.

Future Management: Several excellent pea varieties with multiple resistance to pea and bean viruses are now available. Make use of these varieties if you notice signs of any virus on your peas. Keep in mind that if you have pea enation virus (preceding listing), you will need varieties that are specifically resistant to that disease.

Peach Phony, Peach Decline, Peach Mosaic, and Peach X Viruses

Host Plants: Peach is the only cultivated crop that suffers from this grab bag of viral diseases. These viruses often are hosted by wild fruits including wild plums (in the Southeast) and chokecherries (in the Northeast).

Where It Occurs: Peach phony is widespread in the Southeast, while other viral diseases that causes peaches to decline are common in the Northeast and Southwest.

Vector: In the Southwest, aphids and mites spread viral diseases among peach, plum, cherry, and apricot. In the East and South, leafhoppers are more common vectors.

Making a Diagnosis: The first disease listed, peach phony, is often called peach decline in the Southeast. Over a period of three to five years, new growth is dwarfed and unusually dark green. Trees grow sideways more than upward and produce few if any fruits. Because this disease can be spread by leafhoppers, it is important that home-owners destroy infected trees promptly. Otherwise, your trees may start an epidemic in nearby commercial orchards.

Another virus of peach that causes trees to decline is peach X, which is spread by leafhoppers in the Northeast. Wild chokecherries host this disease. It causes leaves to become speckled and streaked with yellow and red in early summer. The leaves curl upward and appear ragged or tattered. If any fruits are produced, they drop off before they ripen.

Peach mosaic is common in the Southwest. New leaves and stems are dwarfed, and leaves are mottled with yellow. Fruits of peach, nectarine, apricot, and plum trees are small and misshapen.

Immediate Action: Get rid of diseased trees! They will never recover and may become a source of infection for other trees.

Future Management: When buying peach, nectarine, plum, cherry, or apricot trees, pay a little extra for plants that come from reputable nurseries and are certified to be disease free. Many viral diseases are spread during the grafting process. Heavily discounted trees may be of questionable health. Reputable nursery people burn such plants rather than sell them.

Potato Virus Y (PVY), Potato Vein Banding

Host Plants: Potato, tomato, pepper, and several weeds.

Where It Occurs: Especially prevalent in warm climates, but may occur anywhere host plants are grown.

Vector: Many species of aphids.

Making a Diagnosis: This virus may have few symptoms, or may cause light streaks on potato, tomato, and pepper leaves. It is seldom as devastating as other plant viruses, because most plants have some ability to fight back when infected with potato virus Y, often abbreviated at PVY. Leaves with streaks or slight mottling may drop to the ground. On potatoes, this disease is sometimes called potato vein banding, after the way infected leaves develop yellowish cream streaks.

The real problem comes when plants are infected with PVY and another virus, such as tobacco mosaic. In this situation, tomato fruits become mottled and streaked with brown. Pepper production may drop by half, though the plants appear at least marginally healthy. Some of the fruits may show mottling, but plants don't show the leaf distortions characteristic of tobacco mosaic virus.

Immediate Action: Promptly pull up or harvest potatoes that show unusual streaks in leaves, for they may cause later problems if the virus spreads to peppers or tomatoes. Tomatoes that show clear evidence of ongoing viral damage also should be pulled up and buried away from the garden. Peppers normally tolerate this virus rather well and will continue to produce despite infection.

Future Management: This virus can be carried on potato tubers, so inspect your plants carefully before deciding to grow next year's potatoes from this year's crop. Encourage natural aphid predators such as lady beetles and parasitic wasps. If you live near fields where peppers are grown commercially, your peppers face an increased risk of viral diseases. A few varieties are especially tolerant of PVY and other viral diseases.

Raspberry Mosaic Virus, Raspberry Yellow Mosaic

Host Plants: Raspberry and blackberry.

Where It Occurs: Primarily in central and northern states, often occurring on selected varieties.

Vector: Various aphids.

Making a Diagnosis: A gradual decline in the vigor of raspberries over a two- to three-year period often can be attributed to this virus. Leaves show some mottling with dark green, and growth is slower than normal, especially in spring. Leaf edges may curl downward. Berry quality declines. Berries become soft and fall apart easily; they also may be seedy and weak of flavor.

Viruses in the Bramble Patch

In addition to mosaic viruses, raspberries and blackberries are subject to a number of viruses that are barely understood. Since North America is rich in wild strains of these brambles, it is also well endowed with viruses that infect this family of plants. There is often a period of several years between the time a berry is planted and the time it contracts a virus. Plants that slowly decline in vigor, lose berry quality, or set no fruit may be suffering from a virus. When raspberries or blackberries are weakened by viruses, they are easily winterkilled.

Nursery growers often are plagued with these mysterious maladies, which may infect all nursery stock of individual varieties. For example, large numbers of Fallgold raspberry, Cuthbert raspberry, and Darrow blackberry all became infected with obscure viruses during the 1980s. Growers and gardeners had to switch to new varieties.

When brambles are propagated in the normal way, by taking root cuttings or stem cuttings from mature plants, the viruses are easily passed on to the new plants. But nurserymen now have a new tool to use in propagating virus-free plants, called tissue culture. Instead of using a large population of parent plants, an individual virus-free plant can be used to parent hundreds of test-tube babies. Tissue-cultured plants usually cost a little more than others, but they are the surest way to know you are buying plants that host no viruses. The best time to plant them is in spring.

Wild raspberries and blackberries may appear healthy yet host viral diseases that are dangerous to cultivated varieties. To be on the safe side, grow either cultivated or wild berries in your yard — not a mixture of both types. Place cultivated brambles as far from wild ones as you can to discourage infection from disease-carrying aphids as well as various fungal diseases that bother these plants.

A closely related virus, sometimes called raspberry yellow mosaic, also causes leaves to turn yellow. Leaf shape becomes unusually long, and new growth is dwarfed.

Immediate Action: Viruses usually infect berry plants systemically, from the leaf tips to the roots. Once a virus establishes itself in a variety, there is no way to get rid of it but to dig out and destroy the infected plants. Start over with a new variety, but not in exactly the same place where the sick plants were growing.

Future Management: Unless you have wild berries nearby, you can generally eliminate viral problems in brambles by sacrificing diseased plants and establishing a new planting of berries that have no history of disease.

Spotted Wilt Virus

Host Plants: Tomato, pepper, potato, and many flowers and weeds. For vegetable gardeners, tomato is the most susceptible crop.

Where It Occurs: Mostly in the Pacific Coast and Deep South, though summer weather patterns may spread the vectors beyond their normal range.

Vector: Several species of tiny thrips.

Making a Diagnosis: In early summer, just when tomatoes are growing vigorously and starting to set fruit, spotted wilt virus may appear. In some areas it's a threat every year, while in the Mid and Upper South it usually occurs as a cyclical epidemic.

The common symptoms include a sudden proliferation of brown spots on new growth, which may also appear stunted. New growing tips wilt and die. If the plants are holding green fruit, the fruits show ghostly brown or reddish concentric circles and often are rough looking and misshapen. Fruits do not ripen properly.

Immediate Action: If some of your tomatoes are dying of spotted wilt, chances are good that all of your plants have become infected. The best policy is to just wait and see since, in years when this disease is epidemic, there is little a gardener can do to salvage infected tomatoes.

Weather may make it possible to grow a fall crop of tomatoes after the spring crop has been destroyed by spotted wilt. Heavy beating rains kill many thrips. In years when early summer is especially stormy, a second crop of tomatoes set out in late summer may have a fighting chance. Even without beating rains, thrip populations fall off sharply after midsummer, so in areas with long growing seasons you may have luck growing a late tomato crop.

Future Management: Many researchers are working hard to develop resistant varieties, which should become available in coming years. Meanwhile, use reflective mulch or late crops and cross your fingers. The best defense yet found is aluminum reflective mulch material, which confuses the thrips and discourages them from feeding. Floating row covers do little good since the thrips that carry this disease are so small that they can squeeze through many row covers. If you try row covers, wrap them around the outside of tomato cages, or use other methods to keep the fabric from chafing against tomato leaves and growing tips.

Strawberry Stunt and Other Strawberry Viruses

Host Plants: Strawberry.

Where It Occurs: Mostly in the Pacific Northwest. Strawberries are subject to a number of viruses that may develop in places where strawberry aphids are common, or where infected plants are grown.

Vector: Strawberry aphid.

Making a Diagnosis: Strawberry stunt is a syndrome that includes dwarfing of plants, dull, papery leaves with curled-down edges, and thin flower stalks topped by infertile flowers.

Several other strawberry viruses cause plants to be stunted, sometimes with unusual tufts of small leaves emerging from the centers of the plants. There also are mottle and mosaic viruses of strawberry, though they're not as common as the viruses that cause stunting.

Immediate Action: Pull up and destroy affected plants. If only a few plants show symptoms, rogueing of diseased plants may give lasting relief. Yet plants that appear healthy can host the virus, so watch them carefully. When more than a third of the plants in a strawberry bed show signs of viral infection, destroy the whole planting and start over with a new variety in fresh soil.

Future Management: Strawberries are susceptible to many viruses that are transmitted by the strawberry aphid. When planting a new strawberry patch, start with virus-free plants from a reputable dealer. In addition to viruses, many other diseases can be imported on inferior plants.

Few strawberry plantings last forever. Viruses, fungi, and soil-borne rots often become established on strawberries after two to three years. In warm climates, strawberries often are grown as winter annuals to avoid these problems. In more temperate climates, moving strawberries to new soil or starting new plantings with fresh stock at least every five years should maintain bountiful harvests.

Tobacco Etch Virus

Host Plants: Potato, pepper, tomato, and other plants, including petunia.

Where It Occurs: Mostly in warm climates, especially where tobacco is commercially grown.

Vector: Several species of aphids, including peach and bean aphids.

Making a Diagnosis: The symptom that sets tobacco etch apart from other viruses is faint brown spots and scratches that appear in unusual folds and crinkles on leaves. New leaves and old ones develop these brown line patterns, which also may appear on fruits. On peppers, fruits often are small and misshapen, and production is reduced by one-fourth. Plants wilt badly in midday, as this virus also causes some of the plants' roots to die.

Immediate Action: If symptoms appear early in the season, pull up affected plants and compost them. Encourage aphid predators, and cover plants with floating row covers during the first half of summer to limit visits from disease-carrying aphids. This is especially worthwhile if you live near fields where tobacco or peppers are commercially grown, for large plantings often are the source of infections that appear in home gardens.

Future Management: This disease does not persist in seed, but may be hosted by many weeds. Control perennial weeds as best you can. Spray tomato and pepper plants periodically with soapy water to discourage aphids. Several newer pepper varieties are tolerant to tobacco etch virus. Make use of them if this disease is known to be prevalent in your area.

Tobacco Mosaic Virus (TMV)

Host Plants: Tomato, pepper, eggplant, spinach, petunia, tobacco, and numerous weeds.

Where It Occurs: Worldwide.

Vector: Usually humans.

Making a Diagnosis: This virus is found in more gardens than any other, but that does not mean it is easy to identify. Other viruses are associated with feeding by insects that carry the viruses from plant to plant, but insects only transmit TMV by chance, if they happen to pick it up on their mouthparts. It is usually transmitted mechanically by tools, hands, and clothing, and often gets its start when an infected plant or person comes into the garden. Once established, TMV is very difficult to get rid of since it can persist in dead plant material for fifty years.

On tomatoes, symptoms include leaves that have unusual dark and light green mottling. This is easiest to see when the plants are shaded. Leaf edges may be stiff and dry. Plants grow slowly, new leaves are small and crinkled, and plants begin to appear stunted. Fruit set is light, and fruits that do form may have light and dark green mottling accompanied by brown patches. Sick plants wilt during midday more than healthy ones.

Eggplant has similar symptoms, only worse. If infected when young, eggplants often die.

Pepper plants show evidence of TMV in their leaves, which become puckered and mottled with light green or yellow. Leaf veins fade to light yellow. The size of new leaves is reduced, and few blossoms develop. If fruits do set, they are small and misshapen.

Immediate Action: Pull up infected plants and burn them. Do not attempt to replace casualties with new plants, for bits of root left in the soil from diseased plants may lead to immediate infection. When handling diseased plants, work when other plants are dry to reduce the likelihood of spreading this disease. Also avoid brushing against other plants. Wash your hands thoroughly and change your clothes before attending to other garden chores.

Scientists don't know why, but milk seems to act as a neutralizer of the TMV virus. If you know you have TMV but never know where it will turn up, try this approach used by some plant breeders. Whenever you are snipping, pruning, staking, or otherwise working with tomatoes or peppers, fill a bowl with a half-and-half mixture of milk and water. Dip your hands in it every few minutes. Also dip knives or pruning shears in the milk mixture.

Future Management: Guarded, at best. Once TMV has entered your garden, you must constantly be vigilant and very careful to keep it from becoming a monster. Sometimes TMV comes compliments of smokers, because the dried tobacco in cigarettes can carry the virus. You can also import it on contaminated plants or plant containers that came into contact with contaminated plants.

Fortunately, many excellent tomato and pepper varieties are resistant to TMV. If you have seen TMV in your garden, grow only resistant varieties for several years. After a rest period of three or four years, you can try nonresistant varieties if you are very careful not to bruise the plants and watch them very closely. The TMV virus can enter plants through any wound to a leaf, stem, or hair.

◄ CHAPTER 7 ►

NIGHTMARE NEMATODES
Root-Knot, Lesion, and Other Nematodes

Every handful of soil on earth hosts some type of nematode. There are thousands of different kinds, including some that inhabit the bodies of animals. Others live on soil-dwelling insects, while still others live in lakes, ponds, and rivers. Only a relatively few species parasitize plants in a harmful way. These are the nematodes that are of concern to gardeners.

The nematodes that bother gardens are very tiny wormlike organisms, much smaller than bits of thread. The word *nematode* comes from the Greek word *nematos*, meaning thread. Most nematodes can't be seen without the aid of a microscope, for in addition to being small they're often translucent. If you have a microscope that can magnify things to fifty times their size and you look at several different samples of soil, sooner or later you'll see a nematode. At this magnification, they often resemble semicircular fingernail clippings. The largest garden nematodes are ⅛-inch long, while the smaller ones are so tiny that dozens could fit on a coarse grain of sand.

Nematodes exist everywhere but are most numerous in warm climates. They are relatively inactive when temperatures are low. And, while some nematodes have adapted to live in dense clay soil, the comparatively large, open spaces between the soil particles in sandy soil are much more to their liking. The preference for sandy soil probably has to do with the way they move. Nematodes are swimmers and move by slithering from side to side like snakes. They are sometimes called eelworms.

Different nematodes make their way in a variety of settings. Some live in plant stems, while most spend their lives in the soil, seeking out and feeding upon plant roots. The vast majority of the several hundred species of nematodes that parasitize plants work underground. Since people tend to pay more attention to the aboveground parts of plants, gardeners often overlook nematode activity and damage.

Regardless of the climate in which they live, nematode populations are much higher in mid- to late summer than at other times of year. When the soil is cool, nematodes rest. When temperatures are warmer, they proliferate with wild abandon. Some species lay 500 eggs during their lifetimes. The time required for a nematode to grow from hatchling to adult is often less than a month.

Considering these numbers, it's small wonder that nematodes are thought to be responsible for crop losses that rob the human world of up to 10 percent of its food supply. Good thing, then, that nematodes have so many natural enemies. For every nematode that feeds on plants, there is another that feeds on nematodes. In the teeming community of microscopic life in a plot of healthy, biologically active soil, nematodes also may be killed by other small animals, bacteria, or even fungi. Some fungi have the ability to throw out nooselike appendages that trap hapless nematodes, which are then devoured by the fungi.

In the United States nematodes are serious pests, but they are usually much worse in more tropical lands. One of the reasons why slash-and-burn agriculture fails within a few years in tropical settings is the presence of nematodes. Let's say an African farmer clears and cultivates some land, plants a crop, and does well. The next season he plants the same crop again. By the third planting, nematodes that love the crop in question have built up to very damaging numbers. Production topples, and the field is abandoned. Time to go burn off a new field.

The same thing happened when the United States was first colonized and farmed. After a few years of growing cotton or corn, farmers found that the soil got tired. Certainly considerable nutrient depletion had taken place, but the real problem in many cases was probably nematodes combined with diseases that often follow close behind. In addition to the damage done directly by nematode feeding, soilborne wilts and rots increase dramatically since the holes nematodes make in roots are open doors for other pathogens.

These stories introduce the most important aspect of managing any nematode problem, which is to rotate crops. Plants vary in their attractiveness to different nematodes, though most nematodes can feed successfully upon several different plants. By substituting unattractive crops for the ones nematodes like, you can suppress their numbers. Rotations also interrupt the life cycles of the disease-causing organisms that attack plant roots after the nematodes have let them inside.

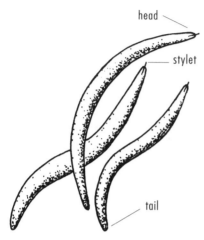

Nematodes resemble very tiny earthworms. All parasitic species have a needlelike appendage at the head end, called a stylet. The stylet is used to pierce cells. Depending on the species, the stylet may be used to emit chemicals that disable plant cells and permit the nematode to enter or as a mouthpiece for sucking cell juices.

Still, it's probably impossible to get rid of any nematode once and for all. Some will always survive in spite of control methods that include chemical fumigation, heat sterilization, and other processes that give temporary relief. If you rotate a crop the nematodes cannot use into nematode-infested soil, some nematodes with starve, but some eggs will lie dormant in the soil, waiting patiently for a host to appear.

Nematode eggs communicate with their host plants in a surprising way. Chemicals released by plant roots give nematode eggs a signal to hatch. When the right chemical message is received, nematode eggs that are several years old may miraculously come to life.

There are five major groups of nematodes of concern to gardeners. These include root-knot nematodes; cyst nematodes; lesion nematodes; a quirky but large group often referred to as stunt, sting, dagger, and needle nematodes; and stem and bulb nematodes, which inhabit plant stems and storage roots, but not small feeder roots. Each of these are examined singly in the entries below.

Major Nematode Groups

Root-Knot Nematodes

Type of Organism: Various species of the *Meloidognye* genus, including M. *halpa*, the northern root-knot nematode, and M. *incognita*, the southern root-knot nematode. M. *javanica* and M. *arenaria* also are important species.

Host Plants: The northern species is a prime pest of strawberry and peanut, as well as leafy greens, cucumber family, tomato, pepper, eggplant, and many flowers. The southern species is barely interested in strawberry or peanut but often devastates peach, okra, bean, watermelon, tomato, pepper, eggplant, and numerous other plants.

Where It Occurs: The northern species inhabits sandy soils in the North, while the southern root-knot nematode is common throughout the Sun Belt and as far north as New Jersey. It, too, survives best in sandy soil.

Making a Diagnosis: When root-knot nematodes invade a plant, they do so by finding a comfortable place in a small root and setting up housekeeping there. Once they get inside a root, they inject several cells with a chemical that causes the cells to become giant. The oversized cells multiply along with normal-sized cells and form a gall, or swelling, on roots. Although some galls thus formed are up to ½-inch across, most are small and scattered, like tiny beads attached to the stringy roots.

Meanwhile, inside the gall the female nematode's body swells and she begins to lay a mass of eggs in a jelly-like material. If conditions are good, these eggs hatch in a few weeks and mature in a month. In Florida, the southern root-knot nematode may produce a dozen generations a year. Because root-knot nematodes don't move far in the soil without human help, frequently some closely spaced plants are attacked, while others at the ends of the row are left unscathed.

Aboveground, you see slightly stunted plants that seem chronically thirsty. If heat stress is severe, leaf tips may curl and turn brown.

With their roots tied up in knots, plants can't take up enough water and nutrients. They often manage to stay alive, but leaves wilt badly in midday sun despite watering, and older leaves slowly turn yellow from nutrient starvation.

To confirm a diagnosis, dig up a struggling plant and examine the roots. In addition to galls protruding from primary or secondary roots, you may see forked root tips. If you're still unsure, replant the suspicious soil with a highly susceptible plant such as strawberry (northern species) or okra (southern species). After a month, root galls should be evident.

When nematodes attack plants, irregular galls form on plant roots and root tips often become forked. The galls may be quite large on plants such as potato or carrot that normally develop fleshy roots. On plants with fibrous roots, the galls are smaller and more widely spaced.

Immediate Action: Gardening in soil inhabited by root-knot nematodes requires constant strategic planning. Here are seven tactics to build into your overall management plan.

▲ **Practice rotation starvation.** In many situations, you can suppress nematodes by alternating susceptible plants with resistant ones. With the northern root-knot species, corn and grains are non-preferred hosts. The southern species avoids dwarf marigolds. By observing the health of plants in your garden, you'll discover other plants that make poor hosts for these nematodes. Whenever you find plants (or individual varieties) that show no evidence of root-knot attack, grow them at every opportunity. Nematodes multiply slowly or not at all when their preferred host plants are absent.

▲ **Keep the soil biologically active.** When you add compost, manure, and other microbially active substances to your garden soil, you increase the diversity of life in the soil's living community. Some of these life forms will be predators of nematodes. In addition, plants benefit from improved soil fertility and texture, so their roots will be healthier to start with. Of particular interest are soil amendments that contain chitin, such as seafood meal, eggshells, shrimp hulls, and the like. When these are added to soil, they stimulate the growth of microorganisms that feed on chitin. Since nematode eggs are coated with chitin, they become victims in this natural process. It's a simple case of exploiting a small ecological niche to your advantage.

▲ **Make use of timed plantings.** Root-knot nematode populations are very high during the second half of summer and much less threatening during winter and early spring. Grow susceptible crops when populations are low and resistant ones when populations are high. In mild winter areas where the southern root-knot nematode is epidemic, you may have surprising luck growing many hardy vegetables and flowers during the winter months.

▲ **Solarize soil in midsummer.** The yearly peak in nematode populations often occurs just when you're ready to replant vegetable and flower beds for your fall garden. In between spring and summer plantings, you can heat up badly infested soil beneath a sheet of clear plastic to kill many nematodes. To solarize, follow the step-by-step directions given on page 23 in Chapter 2. In the Deep South, always solarize before planting fall crops of carrots, onions, turnips, and other susceptible crops.

▲ **Practice good sanitation.** Root-knot nematodes seldom travel more than a few feet from the place where they hatch — unless you give them a ride. There's little danger in walking from place to place on your property, since root-knot nematodes live in rather than on the soil. But you can easily transport them to new beds on tools such as shovels, digging forks, or the tines of your tiller. After working in soil known to be populated by root-knot nematodes, thoroughly clean tools by running them under a hose before moving to a new spot of soil.

Instead of turning under nematode-infested plants, dig them up. Stuff the plants (especially the root portions) into a black or clear plastic bag. Leave the bag in the sun for several days to a week, or until the plants have cooked to death. You can then chop and compost the plants in a hot compost heap (see page 14).

▲ **Grow resistant varieties.** Several varieties of tomatoes, hot peppers, and some other crops are resistant to root-knot nematodes. Use these at every opportunity, both to make sure you get a crop and to frustrate your resident nematodes.

▲ **Mulch and water.** If you grow susceptible plants in nematode-infested soil, you must stand ready to meet their increased need for water. Many plants can tolerate some nematode parasites and still produce well if they are adequately supplied with water. Use mulch to help keep moisture in the soil; biodegradable mulches go a step further by hosting an array of microorganisms, many of whom are beneficial. Even plastic mulches can help in the fight against nematodes. Besides holding soil moisture, they reduce weed competition and the amount of soil splashing that goes on during heavy rainstorms. This in turn reduces the threat of other diseases and the spread of nematodes.

Future Management: You can garden in soil infested with root-knot nematodes, but it's an ongoing challenge. By using the strategies outlined above, you stand a good chance of growing very nice crops of most plants. Still, if you have the space, consider moving your garden periodically and allowing the old garden spot to lie fallow for two or three seasons. This rest period can be very disappointing to nematodes ready and waiting for their next meal.

Cyst Nematodes

Type of Organism: Several species of nematode in the genus *Heterodera*, which includes the golden nematode, cabbage nematode, and sugar beet nematode.

Host Plants: Cyst nematodes are more crop-specific than the root-knot group. The golden nematode is a parasite of potato, tomato, and eggplant. The cabbage and sugar beet species live on the roots of cabbage family crops and leafy greens.

Where They Occur: The golden nematode is limited to the upper mid-Atlantic states, where potatoes are rigorously inspected to keep this rare but long-lived nematode in a state of perpetual quarantine. The cabbage cyst nematode occurs mostly in California. The sugar beet nematode is common wherever sugar beets are grown.

Making a Diagnosis: Cyst nematodes don't actually enter plant roots. Instead, they have an unusually long stylet (mouth needle) that they stick into plant roots. The nematode remains attached as its body swells and produces eggs. The eggs develop inside the body of the dead parent, so the whole mass resembles a cyst attached to plant roots. These cysts are so small that they're very difficult to see but may appear as white or brown specks attached to plant roots.

Plants that are seriously attacked by these nematodes grow poorly, appear stunted, and wilt readily in midday sun. Unrelated plants in the same vicinity may look just fine. In other words, where the golden nematode is active, potatoes and tomatoes may suffer while cucumbers thrive. Peas and beans show a healthy contrast to cabbage-family crops that are being sucked dry by cyst nematodes.

Immediate Action: If you have the misfortune to find yourself trying to garden in soil that was farmed until the space was abandoned due to these nematodes, you may want to strike the most susceptible crops from your planting list temporarily. Grow only non-host plants for two years and then gradually reintroduce the ones the nematodes really want.

Future Management: Although cyst nematode eggs may remain viable in soil for five to fifteen years, their weakness is that all species have a very limited host range. These nematodes seldom cause problems in soil where crops are rotated often. When a gardener is faced with soil infested with cyst nematodes, a few seasons of smart rotations should get them under control.

Lesion Nematodes

Type of Organism: Several species of the genus *Pratylenchus*.

Host Plants: Grains and grasses, tomato, pepper, eggplant, celery, parsley, and several fruits including apple, peach, fig, and strawberry.

Where It Occurs: Individual species are widely distributed throughout warm and temperate climates.

Making a Diagnosis: The symptoms caused by lesion nematodes are similar to those of root-knot nematodes, except for the absence of galls on the roots. Instead, many roots will be absent, as this nematode destroys root cells as it feeds. Many roots are severed, resulting in a root mass that may be less than half the size of a normal plant.

Remaining roots may have tiny brown sores, or lesions. Damage often appears in pockets, in which several adjoining plants are damaged but not the entire row or bed.

Aboveground, plants are stunted, new growth is weak, and old leaves may turn yellow and curl under at the edges. In hot weather, plants can't get enough water. If you dig up such a plant, most of the deep roots appear to have been stripped, and the plant may have tried to make up for this loss by growing a mass of new roots just under the soil line.

Plants damaged by lesion nematodes are very easy prey for other soilborne diseases. As lesion nematodes feed, they create many wounds through which fungi and bacteria may enter.

Immediate Action: Pull up damaged plants and place them in a black or clear plastic bag. Place the bag in the hot sun for a week or so to kill the nematodes and their host. Then compost the plants in a hot compost heap. Replant the space with beans, lettuce, spinach, or some other legume or leafy green.

Lesion nematodes are sometimes called meadow nematodes since they are quite at home living in the roots of many meadow grasses.

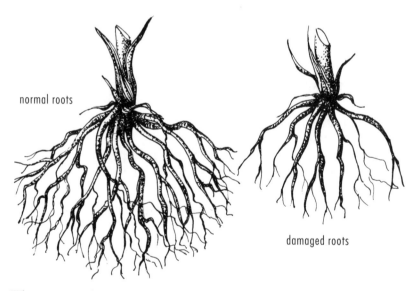

normal roots

damaged roots

When roots are damaged by lesion nematodes, small feeder roots are destroyed and large roots are shortened. Many roots are found close to the soil line, but deeper roots are very sparse.

They don't reproduce as enthusiastically as other nematodes and may be easily brought under control through crop rotation. When establishing new garden space in a previously grassy area, use legumes and leafy greens as cover crops as often as you can.

Future Management: Very good, unless you insist on growing suscep-tible crops year after year in infested soil. Where fruits have suffered from this pest, do not replant the space with new plants until the soil has been cover-cropped with a resistant plant for several seasons. These nematodes can overwinter in dead roots, so it may take two years or more to starve them out.

Stunt, Sting, Dagger, and Needle Nematodes

Type of Organism: Numerous species belonging to several genera, in-cluding *Xiphenema* (dagger nematodes), *Longidorus* (needle nema-todes),and *Trichodorus* (stubby root nematodes).

Host Plants: A wide variety of plants in virtually all plant families.

Where They Occur: Widely distributed throughout the world. Usually occur as problems in isolated geographic pockets. Sandy, porous soils are most likely to host these nematodes.

Making a Diagnosis: The damage caused by these nematodes is remark-ably similar to that caused by Fusarium wilt (page 34), but the plants parasitized by these nematodes usually don't die. Instead, they limp along on skimpy root systems and survive as long as they can take up sufficient water. A bad drought may do them in, but otherwise they grow slowly, often turn yellow, and produce poorly.

The nematodes in this group feed on roots from the outside only, so they do not cause galls or knots to form. However, they may transmit viruses or other diseases as they travel from plant to plant. Little is known about the life cycles of these nematodes, or about their host plant preferences. Some species cause serious damage to certain plants, but they may be equally satisfied sucking root juice from an unrelated plant.

Immediate Action: Only a very unusual garden hosts these nematodes. Farmers who grow the same plants year after year set the scene for a buildup of these parasites, but diversified home gardens carry a very low risk of infection.

Should you find that the roots of some plants are terribly skimpy and you rule out other plant diseases, take the same steps you would for other nematodes. Pull up and kill the host plants by leaving them in the sun in a plastic bag, and replant the garden space with an unrelated crop. Yet bear in mind that these nematodes live in soil and not in plants. They are most numerous in the soil *around* plants, but never enter roots except to stick in their needle-noses to refresh themselves.

Future Management: Excellent, since it is unlikely that a gardener would have problems with these nematodes in the first place. Intensive rotation should solve any problem that does develop. Maintaining biologically active soil is also a prime defensive strategy. In dire situations, the ultimate weapon against these nematodes is soil solarization.

Stem and Bulb Nematodes

Type of Organism: Several species of the genus *Ditylenchus*.

Host Plants: More than 400 types of plants, including beans and peas, corn, onion, strawberry, grains, and flower bulbs.

Where It Occurs: Primarily in temperate climates where plant tissue doesn't fully rot during the winter. Some species also occur in semitropical areas.

Making a Diagnosis: The symptoms caused by these nematodes resemble those of several other plant diseases. They are most likely to occur during or just after very rainy weather, as these nematodes travel in water to invade tender plant tissues starting from the roots, stems, or tender young leaves. They are especially talented at colonizing young seedlings. When seedlings are invaded, they become stunted, twisted, and yellowed. Frequently small galls or bumps develop on the main stems. Bulbs become spongy and soft.

When considering the possibility of stem nematodes, keep in mind that these nematodes prefer stems to roots. They choke plants by clogging up stems with their bodies and destroying interior stem cells. Therefore, the roots of plants damaged by stem nematodes often appear normal.

Immediate Action: Pull up damaged plants and place them in a black or clear plastic bag; place the bag in hot sun for a week or so to kill the nematodes and their host. In cool weather, place rogued plants in a large bucket and douse with boiling water. Temperatures above 115°F (46°C) kill these nematodes. Some bulbs can be saved by placing them in hot water for an hour. However, the water temperature must be closely monitored, for if the water is too hot the bulbs will also be killed.

Long rotations will also help bring stem nematodes under control. Leafy greens, potatoes, and carrots are usually resistant. Soil solarizations (see page 23 in Chapter 2) also is a viable option.

Future Management: Very good with annual plants, since rotations are simple to implement with annuals. As these nematodes don't reproduce as aggressively as most others, you should be able to suppress them even when growing perennials by using compost and mulch to keep soil biologically active.

◀ CHAPTER 8 ▶

GREAT MASQUERADERS
Common Plant Problems that Resemble Diseases

Not every leaf that becomes crinkled or fruit that sports speckles is troubled by disease. Several other likely causes include insects, nutritional disorders, weather extremes, and various forms of pollution. Each of these possibilities is discussed below, along with appropriate remedies.

INSECT DAMAGE THAT LOOKS LIKE DISEASE

When an insect feeds on a plant, most of the time you can see quite clearly what's going on. Caterpillars whose colors camouflage nicely within leafy canopies leave behind a telltale trail of excrement. Various beetle larvae that eat or skeletonize leaves are easily found by peeking under the damaged leaves. Sometimes you must wait until night and do your peeking with a flashlight, but sooner or later you'll find the hungry offenders.

Yet there are some insects whose feeding activities are so well concealed that you may find yourself wondering whether you're looking at an insect or a disease. Some insects are so small and fast moving that they hide before you can identify them. Others feed underground, inside plants, or only at night, so they're seldom seen.

If you've looked through the chart, "Symptoms of Diseases of Vegetables and Fruits" (Chapter 9) and can't match up the symptoms you see with a disease, consider the types of insect injury described in the table below. These often appear to be diseases at first glance.

Is It a Disease or an Insect?
Symptoms of Common Insect Damage

FLEA BEETLES

SYMPTOM

Numerous tiny, very slightly puckered holes make the leaf look like it was fired upon with miniature buckshot; edges of holes may be pale gray or brown.

PLANTS AFFECTED

Eggplant, leafy greens (especially mustard), tomato, pepper, petunia, corn, sweetpotato, okra, radish, southern pea.

WHAT TO DO

Tolerate light damage (always worst in early to mid- spring); delay planting until late spring when possible; protect arugula, eggplant, and other highly susceptible plants with floating row covers.

LEAFHOPPERS

SYMPTOM

Leaf tips and edges turn brown and curl under.

PLANTS AFFECTED

Beans, potato, some flowers.

WHAT TO DO

Apply soap spray (insecticidal soap) to both sides of leaves, repeat after one week.

LEAF MINERS

SYMPTOMS

Pale meandering trails in leaves that look like leaves have been scribbled on.

PLANTS AFFECTED

Leafy greens such as spinach and Swiss chard; pepper; southern pea; many flowers, especially columbine.

WHAT TO DO

Pick off and destroy disfigured leaves, encourage parasitic wasps, cover plants with floating row cover.

Nocturnal Beetles, Japanese Beetles

SYMPTOMS

Clean-edged irregular holes in leaves appear overnight.

PLANTS AFFECTED

Beans, okra, bramble fruits, rose, others.

WHAT TO DO

Check at night with flashlight to confirm the problem; handpick at night, dust with sabadilla, or tolerate damage.

Plant Bugs

SYMPTOMS

Young leaves and growing tips show small brown dots.

PLANTS AFFECTED

Many flowers, herbs, spring greens.

WHAT TO DO

Tolerate damage, use floating row covers, or dust with sabadilla.

Root Maggots

SYMPTOMS

Young plants suddenly wilt and die.

PLANTS AFFECTED

Onion, cabbage family.

WHAT TO DO

Rotate crops; use floating row covers in early spring.

Scale

SYMPTOMS

Fruit tree branches gummy, with bunches of small flat discs.

PLANTS AFFECTED

Mostly fruits, houseplants.

WHAT TO DO

In winter, clean bark with a soft brush; follow with dormant oil spray.

SPIDER MITES

SYMPTOMS

Leaves pale yellow with some green remaining, as though airbrushed with green.

PLANTS AFFECTED

Squash family, beans, strawberry, flowers, houseplants.

WHAT TO DO

Drench plants with insecticidal soap, then cover with a light blanket to block out light and maintain high moisture level. Lift covers after three days, wait a few days, and repeat the treatment.

SQUASH BUGS, STINK BUGS, AND OTHER SHIELD BUGS

SYMPTOMS

Tiny beige or brown angular spots, from as small as a pinprick up to ¼ inch.

PLANTS AFFECTED

Squash, cucumber, melon, okra, beans, southern pea, tomato.

WHAT TO DO

Handpick adults; look for and destroy eggs; dust plants with sabadilla.

THRIPS

SYMPTOMS

Small, closely spaced white to silvery spots or streaks on plant leaves.

PLANTS AFFECTED

Cabbage, lettuce, onion, okra, southern pea, many flowers.

WHAT TO DO

Tolerate light damage; spray leaf undersides with insecticidal soap.

If you want to learn more about how to understand and control garden insects, consult one of two buggy companions to this book. *The Gardener's Bug Book*, by Barbara Pleasant (Storey Publishing, 1994), gives detailed life cycle information about harmful and beneficial garden insects plus controls. *Bugs, Slugs & Other Thugs*, by Rhonda Massingham Hart (Storey Publishing, 1991) gives control options for problems with rodents, pets, wild animals, and mollusks, as well as insects.

NUTRITIONAL DISORDERS THAT LOOK LIKE DISEASES

If you pay close attention to how your garden grows, you may know intuitively when plants are having trouble feeding themselves. Unlike diseases and insects, which usually affect closely spaced groups of like plants or even individual specimens, nutritional problems may affect the whole garden. Or you may see problems in a bed at one end of your yard and no noticeable difficulties at the other end.

Too Sweet or Too Sour?

When plants are malnourished, they usually fail to grow well. Some crops do well in poor soil, including leaf lettuce, bush beans, herbs, and most wildflowers. However, few plants will grow well if the pH — the relative alkalinity/acidity of the soil — is way out of whack. An inappropriate pH sabotages the chemical tricks that plant roots use to turn even high-quality nutrition sources, such as compost or manure, into usable plant food.

The degree of acidity in soil is measured on the pH scale. Within the neutral range, roughly 6.0 to 7.0, most plants grow well. Extremely acidic soils show a lower pH reading, and very alkaline soils show higher readings. Geographically, most soils in the northern two-thirds of the country tend to be slightly acidic. Highly alkaline soils are found mostly in the Southwest and in geographic pockets in the Deep South.

Measuring your soil's approximate pH is easy. Most garden supply stores sell pH test kits for a few dollars. You take a small amount of soil, mix it with the solution provided, and let the mixture settle. Then compare the color of the clear liquid to the color chart that comes in the kit. After testing several samples from your yard, you'll have a good idea of your soil's natural pH tendencies.

If your soil's pH is extremely high or low, get to work putting things right. If you don't, plants won't be able to uptake needed nutrients even if those nutrients are present in the soil, ready and waiting to be used.

For acidic soil, the first step is to work in a dusting of dolomitic limestone or agricultural lime. Lime needs a few months to raise a pH that's too low; lime applied in fall will usually have noticeable impact by the following spring. Acidic clay soils rarely need liming more

Fixing Nitrogen-Fixing Legumes

Beans and peas use special bacteria, called rhizobia, to help them convert nitrogen from the air into a usable nutrient. When legumes are operating efficiently, they temporarily store this nitrogen in small nodules on their roots and then use the stored nitrogen when they begin to develop seeds.

Few soils contain high levels of these rhizobia on their own, and the situation is further complicated by the fact that different types of legumes use different types of rhizobia. Over time, by growing legumes over and over, your garden soil will accumulate enough of these beneficial microorganisms so that it can be considered self-inoculating. However, when you're growing any legume in new garden soil for the first time, you'll get a much better crop if you take a few minutes to inoculate the seeds with a powdered inoculant.

Keep in mind that these soil rhizobia are constantly being killed by other soil microorganisms, cold weather, and starvation (when no host plants are present). If you live where the soil freezes hard every winter, it's a good idea to inoculate legumes every year. Soil that hasn't been gardened for several years also needs to have deposits made in its rhizobial bank.

Most garden supply stores and mail order seed companies sell all-purpose legume inoculant that contains a mixture of rhizobia that meets the needs of all beans and peas. You put some of the powder in a jar or plastic bag, add the seeds, and shake.

When uninoculated peas, beans, or other legumes are grown where no similar crop has been grown before, they need more soil nitrogen since they cannot fix much for themselves.

than every other year, since water and nutrients percolate through them slowly. Sandy soils that are extremely acidic often require annual treatments with lime.

Never add lime to alkaline soils, because it will only make the situation worse. Instead, concentrate on enriching the soil with rotted leaves, peat moss, and other forms of organic matter. In general, fully decomposed tree by-products (sawdust, leaf mold, rotted bark) are acidic, so they are very desirable amendments for alkaline soil.

Pine needles make an excellent mulch and slowly acidify the soil underneath.

Alkaline soil also may be treated with powdered sulfur, a naturally occurring mineral that lowers the soil's pH. To apply sulfur, dust the soil very lightly and then cultivate. Use about a pound (0.5 kilogram) for each 100 square feet (9 square meters). When preparing planting holes in alkaline soil for long-lived trees or small fruits, dig the holes several weeks ahead of time and mix a cup or so of sulfur into the soil (along with copious amounts of fully rotted organic matter) as you backfill the hole.

Keeping Plants Well-Fed

Once your soil's pH tendencies have been identified and corrected (if needed), it's time to look at other fertility factors. You can have your soil tested through your Extension Service or use a soil test kit to do it yourself. Or you can grow spinach. In my experience, any soil that will grow good spinach will grow just about anything.

There is some danger in trusting soil test data over what you actually see going on in your garden. Soil isn't uniform, and the portion(s) you tested may not reflect your entire garden. If you are continuously adding compost, manure, leaf mold, grass clippings, and other forms of organic matter to your soil, it should be in excellent shape after three years. Organic matter acts as a sponge to hold nutrients where plants can get them easily. But if you keep piling on chemical fertilizers when you already have good soil (or instead of adding organic matter), you may end up with soil that can't keep a steady pH and plants that are rank yet produce poorly.

For most gardeners, simply enriching beds once a year with a thick blanket of compost or manure, using biodegradable mulches, and growing cover crops from time to time will maintain acceptable levels of soil fertility (see page 12). Still, few soils are well endowed with everything, so you should also be on the lookout for spot shortages of certain nutrients.

Most nutritional deficiencies can be treated in the short run by drenching plants with a fish emulsion/kelp mixture. The fish component provides nitrogen, while the kelp serves a banquet of micronutrients. If plants are seriously malnourished, you should see definite results after two applications spaced five days apart. Before planting another crop in such soil, take definite steps to improve its tilth and fertility with rich organic matter such as rotted manure.

"Diseases" Caused by Calcium Deficiency

So far, we've discussed problems plants develop when certain nutrients are in short supply, or when plants are unable to use nutrients because of extremes in soil pH. Now let's consider some common problems that emerge when weather patterns come into play. Two common vegetable garden problems — blossom end rot and tipburn — appear to be diseases but are really calcium uptake disorders that develop when certain weather patterns prevail.

Blossom end rot of tomato and bell pepper is the most common one. This disorder is characterized by large or small black spots on the blossom (bottom) end of tomato fruits. Spots gradually become larger and rot. Blossom end rot often develops in midseason, when weather changes from wet and mild to hot and dry. You may pick a large crop of perfect fruits and then find that subsequent harvests in late summer are marred by blossom end rot.

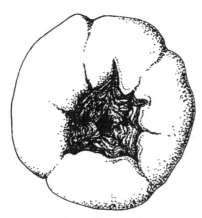

Blossom end rot of tomato is not a disease, but a calcium uptake disorder.

To minimize damage from this disorder, keep tomatoes heavily mulched so that the soil stays constantly moist. When the risk of blossom end rot is high (when the second "set" of green fruits coincides with the onset of hot, dry weather), try spritzing plants with a seaweed product to help meet their nutrient needs. When weather forces have the upper hand and blossom end rot develops in spite of your efforts, pick off affected fruits promptly to encourage the plants to continue blossoming and setting new fruits.

The same weather pattern that causes blossom end rot of tomato can lead to blossom end rot of summer squash. But since summer squashes mature so quickly, the best intervention is simply to snip off fruits that have shriveled blossom ends and then water the plants well.

Potatoes, lettuce, and other leafy vegetables may show a symptom called tipburn when they're having problems getting enough

Clues to Identifying Malnourished Plants

A quick look at any plant growing in poor soil tells its own story, but occasionally plants show strange symptoms associated with restricted availability of specific nutrients. Here are a few clues to common nutritional deficiencies in garden plants, and what to do if you see them.

Major Nutrient Deficiencies

▲ **Nitrogen** — Light green leaves, slow growth, and slightly smaller size indicate too little nitrogen, while very robust, dark green leaves and few blossoms indicate too much. Manure, blood meal, cottonseed meal, alfalfa meal, fish meal, and many other soil amendments supply nitrogen. Grow legume cover crops and incorporate composted manure into soil to keep nitrogen levels in the normal range.

▲ **Phosphorous** — Unusual purplish streaks in corn leaves and stems, purple coloring on tomato leaf veins or leaf undersides, and other plants showing the color purple in unusual places may indicate too little phosphorous. Soil that receives regular infusions of compost should not be deficient, but you can easily eliminate this risk by scattering bone meal or rock phosphate into the soil every few years.

▲ **Potassium** — If squash or beet leaves show a bronze cast, or strawberries grow slowly and show purple in their leaves, your soil could be low in this major nutrient. Compost, manure, and other organic soil amendments may solve the problem, or you can apply granite dust or greensand to the soil in fall every few years. Save wood ashes from your fireplace to treat spot shortages.

▲ **Magnesium** — Yellow peanut leaves, red or orange or purplish color in older leaves of many plants, and drying and browning of leaf tips or edges are all symptoms of magnesium deficiency. Some soils are naturally low in this mineral. If a soil test indicates a problem, use dolomitic limestone to correct it. Until the limestone takes effect (usually several months), spray plants with a seaweed or kelp foliar spray. If your soil is alkaline, skip the lime-stone and keep heaping on the compost, supplemented with foliar seaweed sprays.

Micronutrient Deficiencies

▲ **Iron** — The pale green or yellowish leaves usually associated with low nitrogen may instead indicate too little iron, especially when plants are growing in alkaline soil. Raspberries, strawberries, beets, and many other plants show yellow leaves when they can't get enough iron.

To correct the problem in alkaline soil, bring soil into the normal pH range by adding acidic organic amendments such as rotted leaves or peat moss to the soil. Use sulfur around established fruit trees (follow label recommendations). Add greensand to compost before using it to boost its iron content. In this case, correcting the pH is more important than adding the nutrient that appears deficient; usually the iron is already present in the soil but is tied up by improper pH.

▲ **Manganese** — Yellow splotches in leaves of cucumbers, squash, beets, and other plants may indicate a manganese defi-ciency, which is most common in alkaline soils. Correcting the pH may solve the problem, since this trace nutrient may be present but unavailable to plants in soils where the pH is too high.

▲ **Boron** — Brown spots inside sweetpotatoes and skin blisters outside, black areas inside beets, broccoli with hollow stems, or purple leaf veins in potato often indicate a shortage of this trace element. Some soils that lack organic matter are also low in boron. To correct the problem, use plenty of compost, or sprinkle very small amounts of household borax into soil. Use only 1 teaspoon per 9 square feet (1 square meter) bed, as too much boron causes many more problems than too little.

▲ **Zinc** — When leaves of cherry, grape, or other plants appear unusually small, and they're growing in alkaline soil that has been managed for a long time using only chemical fertilizers, you may be looking at a zinc deficiency. Correcting pH or adding manure is the answer.

calcium and potassium. Typically, they have no problem as long as the weather stays cloudy and damp but react to the sudden onset of bright, sunny weather by showing brown, shriveled areas on the tips of leaves. If the soil in which these plans are growing is adequate, they'll move past this temporary problem and produce quite well.

Should you see tipburn year after year on your potatoes and lettuce, enrich the soil with compost to which a liberal sprinkling of bone meal has been added before planting these crops. While weather is beyond your control, you can easily supplement your soil to improve its ability to provide enhanced sustenance to plants under stress.

TOO COLD OR TOO HOT?

Peas love cool weather, but when plants that are better than knee high endure several nights of near-freezing temperatures, leaves may temporarily turn a sickly yellow color. When the cold weather departs, normal leaf color returns. Even the most cold-hardy plants may suffer frost burn if they're not quite ready when cold weather strikes. Leaves of broccoli, cauliflower, lettuce, and other vegetables grown in spring or fall may show scorched patches on their leaves following frosty weather, but they usually outgrow this damage when mild weather returns.

Very hot temperatures may cause leaves to become curled and scorched, which can lead to other problems. For example, if tomatoes or peppers don't have enough leaves to shade the fruits, the fruits may become marked with pale patches that fail to ripen. This condition is called sunscald, and it looks very much like a disease. If you often see this condition develop in midsummer, drape old sheets or shadecloth (the sheer polyester fabric used to cover greenhouses) over plants during dry heat waves. Also, avoid growing varieties with dark-colored fruits, like purple peppers and black tomatoes (yes, they do exist). These dark colors cause the fruits to heat up and sunscald much worse than yellow, pink, or red fruits.

Among flowers, you may find that varieties with reddish leaves tend to wilt and sunburn much worse than those with light green leaves. Again, the problem is a solar one. Generally, plants with purplish leaves need more shade, as do plants whose leaves are variegated with white.

Trees also have a solar problem in some climates. Young fruit tree trunks in particular are subject to sunscald when their chilled or frozen trunks are suddenly warmed by bright sun. The hot side of the trunk (the south or west side) then splits, and a permanent wound is formed in the tree's most important body part. To keep young trees from becoming permanently weakened by sunscald, wrap the trunks with burlap strips or hardware cloth every fall until the trees have been in the ground for four or five years. After that, a coat of white latex paint will reflect enough light to keep the bark from splitting.

CHEMICAL COMPLICATIONS

As plants interact with the soil, water, and air that surrounds them, they sometimes can be damaged by chemicals they encounter in the environmental arena. Frequently chemical or environmental injury looks like a disease, but its true cause may be discovered with a little detective work. A few problem chemicals are discussed below.

Plant-to-Plant Combat

Many plants, large and small, claim the space in which they grow as their own by releasing chemicals into the soil that discourage the growth of other plants. Scientists call these allelopathic chemicals. Inquiry into exactly what they are and how they work is proceeding fast, but plant allelopathy remains full of unanswered questions. A decade from now, it's possible that commercial herbicides (weed killers) may be based on the natural chemicals that plants use to keep other plants from growing.

Already, several plants are known to have potent allelopathic talents. Walnut trees emit a chemical from their roots that is toxic to tomatoes and many other plants. Maple trees use a similar trick, and some grasses, especially Bermuda and Johnson grass, use chemicals to make the soil inhospitable to peaches, berries, and many other plants.

Where an allelopathic influence is strong, plants will fail to grow well and may die. Their root health is very poor, and they often wilt badly on hot days. In one experiment, three-year-old peach trees grown in Bermuda grass were only half the size of trees grown in rows free of the grass.

In your garden, watch for signs of unwanted influence from nearby trees and from plants that grow close together. In situations in which plants simply refuse to grow and most other factors (soil quality, disease, and insects) can be ruled out, consider the possibility that a super-strong plant is trying to poison a weaker one.

Bad Water

Many common chemicals are water soluble. When they are mixed into water, and that contaminated water is taken up by plants, the plants may suddenly get sick. What looks like a disease may really be a case of bad water.

Two common chemicals, salt and chlorine, are often the cause of plant injury. In dry, arid climates, salt sometimes accumulates naturally in soils. When salt levels become high, the plants are unable to grow well. Similarly, plants grown near saltwater are often subject to salt injury from salt spray. In an urban environment, use of rock salt to keep sidewalks and driveways from icing in winter often causes plants to pickle. The latter form of salt injury can be prevented if you switch to using sand and muscle to get rid of ice in close proximity to shrubs, flowers, or vegetable beds. Save the salt for emergencies, and use it sparingly.

Also be very careful when using cleaning products outdoors to scrub down porches, windows, patios, and other surfaces. Most cleansers that kill mildew contain strong acids or chlorine bleach, which are very dangerous to plants. I have seen lovely patio gardens ruined when their owners cleaned their outdoor furniture and let the rinse water drain into nearby beds. When poisoned by too much chlorine, plant leaves turn yellow and drop off.

The Need for Clean Air

Finally we come to a plant-disease masquerader that is almost always beyond a gardener's control. Plants wear their lungs on their leaves, literally, and can be damaged permanently when exposed to badly polluted air.

This does not have to be "dirty" pollution like smog, though smog can certainly injure plants. Invisible pollutants, such as the gas that escapes from broken gas lines, also can cause leaves to suddenly wither and die. In addition, toxic clouds from factory accidents can conceivably create a situation that looks like plants have been stricken by a foliar disease. If your garden adjoins a field where herbicides are used for weed control, it's possible that chemicals from the field will drift into your property.

When plants are distressed by bad air, the leaves usually become somewhat bleached in appearance. Some herbicides cause stem walls to rupture, but most often herbicides cause established plants to die very slowly.

CONCLUSION

Clearly, there are many things that can go wrong when it comes to growing healthy plants. But more things can go right than can go wrong. Because plants are living things whose main objective in life is to mature and make many offspring, they tend to endure against formidable odds.

As gardeners, as long as we build healthy soil and strive to grow the right plants in the right places at the right time, we can expect excellent success. It's also important to accept the fact that plants get old and die. Whether plant problems come from diseases, weather, or environmental influences, older plants can't cope as well as younger ones. When very old plants die from diseases, they are really dying of natural causes.

◀ CHAPTER 9 ▶

WHAT'S AILING MY GARDEN?
A Quick-Reference Table to Diseases Affecting Common Garden Crops

Use the following alphabetical list of common garden crops and the diseases that bother them to quickly find the most likely causes of trouble in your garden. Then turn to the individual disease entries for more details on identifying the disease and how to respond to the problem.

In situations where varieties are widely available that resist the disease, abbreviations commonly used in seed catalogs also are given. Still, read catalog descriptions carefully, for disease abbreviations may vary from one catalog to the next. And, when a variety is described as "mildew resistant" or simply "disease resistant," it usually means the most common diseases that threaten that crop.

The name of the plant family is included to help you in planning rotations. Since many diseases only infect members of the same family, switching from one family to another can thwart potential disease problems.

Also included are brief healthy plant tips for growing specific garden plants which highlight the most important gardening steps to follow.

APPLE · Rosaceae

DISEASE	SYMPTOMS
Apple Scab	Corky patches on fruit, often at the stem end.
Crown Gall	Corky globular growths on stems, with stunted new growth.
Fire Blight	Young twigs and attached leaves blacken and die; shrunken cankers appear on larger stems.
Lesion Nematodes	Plants spindly, cannot tolerate drought, with thrifty root systems; high risk of secondary root-rot diseases.
Powdery Mildew	Leaves and/or fruits covered with white powder, especially in late summer.

HEALTHY PLANT TIPS
Choose a variety that requires the right number of chill hours for your climate. Monitor soil pH and keep it slightly acidic. Prune annually in late winter; follow pruning with a dormant oil spray to control insects.

APRICOT · Rosaceae

DISEASE	SYMPTOMS
Brown Rot	Fruits become covered with brown mold as they ripen; shrunken mummified fruits hang on trees.
Crown Gall	Corky globular growths on stems; stunted new growth.
Peach Mosaic Virus	New stems dwarfed, leaves mottled with yellow; fruits small and misshapen.

HEALTHY PLANT TIPS
Apricots tend to bloom in early spring and may have trouble holding their blossoms where late freezes are common. Fruit ripens all at once. Handle like small peach trees.

ASPARAGUS   *Liliaceae*

DISEASE	SYMPTOMS
Fusarium Wilt	Plants grow slowly, roots rot; older growth turns yellow and dies.
Gray Mold (Botrytis)	Spear tips spotted with cottony gray mold just as they emerge in spring.

HEALTHY PLANT TIPS

Use raised beds where drainage is questionable. Remove dead foliage and old mulch in winter; replace with a layer of compost mixed with a little soil. Fertilize in late spring with rotted manure or a slow-release organic fertilizer.

BEAN   *Leguminosae*

DISEASE	SYMPTOMS
Anthracnose	Black sores on young stems at soil line; on older plants leaves, stems, and pods have ugly black sores.
Bean Mosaic Virus (BMV, CBMV)	New leaves small, stiff, and yellow; older leaves curled and mottled with yellow.
Curly Top Virus (CTV)	New leaves in dense tuft with curled-down edges; may flower profusely but in vain.
Fusarium Wilt (F)	Plants grow slowly, wilt on hot days, older leaves turn yellow; small fibrous roots rot.
Halo Blight (HB)	Small brown leaf spots surrounded by light green halo; new growth stunted and crinkled.
Powdery Mildew (PM)	Leaves sprinkled with flourlike white powder; plants lose vigor.
Root-Knot Nematodes	Plants grow slowly, can't tolerate drought, show knobby galls on roots.
Soft Rot	Cottony white mold on pods and stems following periods of cool, wet weather.

BEAN (continued)

Stem Nematodes

Seedlings develop bumps on stems and grow very slowly or die.

Rust

Small white blisters on leaf under sides gradually turn orange; leaves turn brown and drop off.

HEALTHY PLANT TIPS

Rotate with nonlegumes, inoculate seeds, and avoid growing in very hot or very cold weather. Generally easy and trouble-free.

BEET AND SWISS CHARD   *Chenopodiacaea*

DISEASE

SYMPTOMS

Cercospora Leaf Spot

Leaves and stems speckled with brown spots; some yellowing between spots.

Curly Top Virus

Leaf veins thick and pale; new growth twisted; small feeder roots look like finely curled hair.

Cyst Nematodes

Plants grow slowly, can't tolerate drought, show stunted roots and don't produce well.

White Rust

Light blisters on leaf undersides that erupt and exude chalky white powder.

HEALTHY PLANT TIPS

Grow in spring and summer when weather is mild. Use neutral soil (pH 7). Not difficult to grow, but these vegetables need regular water to mature quickly.

BLACKBERRY   *Rosaceae*

DISEASE

SYMPTOMS

Anthracnose

Leaf spots with depressed centers, become much worse in wet weather; fruit rots from numerous small sores.

Crown Gall

Corky globular growths on canes, stunted new growth.

Double Blossom Rosette

Blooms lopsided and misshapen with leaflets inside, often in clusters; reduced fruit set.

Gray Mold (Botrytis)

Ripening fruit covered with cottony gray mold.

Raspberry Mosaic Virus

Slow growth, mottled leaves with curled down edges; poor fruit quality and low production.

Rust

Orange deposits on leaf undersides; leaves die and drop off.

HEALTHY PLANT TIPS

Trellis trailing varieties; prune back tips of upright varieties to boost production. Buy new plants from reputable nurseries to assure disease-free start.

BLUEBERRY   *Ericaceae*

DISEASE

SYMPTOMS

Brown Rot (Mummy Berry)

Berries shrivel, darken, and hang on plants as mummies.

Gray Mold (Botrytis)

In wet, cool spring, blossoms turn brown and may be covered with gray cottony mold.

HEALTHY PLANT TIPS

Grow only in acid soil (pH 5–6). Regular watering or irrigation may be needed. Mulch heavily to reduce weed competition and conserve soil moisture. Prune if needed to promote good air circulation.

CABBAGE FAMILY   *Cruciferae*

Cabbage, broccoli, cauliflower, kohlrabi, collard, mustard, turnip, kale, Chinese cabbage, bok choi

DISEASE	SYMPTOMS
Black Rot	V-shaped brown spots on leaves, stunted or lopsided growth, premature death.
Blackleg	Wilting leaves; soft discolored spot on the main stem at the soil line that gradually gets larger.
Cauliflower Mosaic Virus	New leaves small and curled; older ones mottled with yellow and dark green.
Cyst Nematodes	Plants grow slowly, can't tolerate drought, show stunted roots with high incidence of secondary root-rot diseases.
Damping-Off	Seedlings fall over and die during their first month of life.
Downy Mildew (DM)	Brown patches on leaf tops mirrored by fuzzy sections on leaf undersides.
Fusarium Wilt (FY)	Older leaves turn yellow; plants grow very little or wilt to death.
Soft Rot	White cottony mold over wet, rotting spots followed by hard, dark chunks that resemble mouse droppings.
White Rust	Light blisters on leaf undersides that erupt and exude chalky white powder.

HEALTHY PLANT TIPS

Schedule plantings so they mature in cool weather, because low temperatures improve flavor. Mulch, provide adequate water, and rotate with unrelated vegetables.

CARROT   Umbelliferae

DISEASE	SYMPTOMS
Alternaria Blight	Older leaves speckled with brown spots, which run together until leaves shrivel entirely.

CARROT *(continued)*

Aster Yellows

New leaves small and yellow, in tight bunches; roots bulge at top, with curly root hairs.

Cercospora Leaf Spot

Young leaves and stems speckled with brown spots, with some yellowing between spots.

Root-Knot Nematodes

Plants grow slowly, can't tolerate drought, show knobby galls on distorted roots.

Soft Rot

Leaves rot off as white cottony mold develops on tops of roots.

HEALTHY PLANT TIPS

Carrots grow better in sandy or loamy soils than rocky soil or chunky clay; raised beds can help if soil is imperfect. Avoid growing carrots in very hot weather.

CELERY   *Umbelliferae*

DISEASE

SYMPTOMS

Aster Yellows

Inner stalks small, twisted, with brown cracks and yellow color.

Fusarium Wilt

Plants lose vigor, split, become brittle, taste watery and bitter, later rot.

Lesion Nematodes

Plants spindly, can't tolerate drought, root systems stunted; high risk of secondary root-rot diseases.

Septoria Leaf Spot

Yellow speckles on leaves turn gray; gray streaks develop in stems.

Soft Rot

White cottony mold develops as plants turn pinkish and quickly rot.

HEALTHY PLANT TIPS

Garden-grown celery is darker green and less plump than the market version, but it has excellent flavor. Celery needs a long period of mild weather and plenty of water.

CHERRY   *Rosaceae*

DISEASE	SYMPTOMS
Brown Rot	Fruits become covered with brown mold as they ripen; shrunken mummified fruits hang on trees.
Crown Gall	Corky globular growths on stems, stunted new growth.
Peach Mosaic Virus	New stems dwarfed, leaves mottled with yellow; fruits small and misshapen.
Powdery Mildew	Leaves and/or fruits covered with white powder, especially in late summer.

HEALTHY PLANT TIPS

Choose a variety with appropriate chill requirements for your area. Cherries bloom and fruit very early, and may be damaged by late frosts. They are generally easy to grow.

CORN   *Gramineae*

DISEASE	SYMPTOMS
Corn Smut	Sweet corn ears become grossly distorted as kernels turn into monstrous gray blobs; stems sometimes affected.
Lesion Nematodes	Plants spindly, can't tolerate drought, root systems stunted; high risk of secondary root-rot diseases.
Maize Chlorotic Dwarf Virus (MCD)	Severe stunting; new leaves yellow with red streaks.
Maize Dwarf Mosaic Virus (MDM)	Plants short and bushy; pale streaks in leaves.
Northern Corn Leaf Blight (NCLB)	Long, ½-inch-wide tan streaks, starting on lower leaves.
Rust	Short brown streaks in leaves are orange on undersides.

Southern Corn Leaf Blight (SCLB)	Irregular oval tan spots, starting on lower leaves and spreading rapidly in hot, wet weather.
Stem Nematode	Seedlings develop bumps on stems and grow very slowly or die.
Stewart's Wilt (Bacterial Wilt) (SW)	Dwarfed plants with pale creamy streaks on leaves.

HEALTHY PLANT TIPS

Sow as early as possible to avoid major insect pests and diseases. In cold climates, look for varieties that germinate in cold soil. If needed, thin plants to proper spacing.

CUCUMBER FAMILY (CURCUBITS)   *Cucurbitaceae*

Cucumber, winter squash, summer squash, pumpkin, gourd, watermelon, muskmelon, other melons

DISEASE	SYMPTOMS
Angular Leaf Spot (ALS)	Angular spots appear near leaf veins; spot centers turn brown and drop out.
Anthracnose	Watermelons, cucumbers, or sometimes muskmelons have dark brown leaf spots, which become holes. Fruits have soft sunken spots and lack flavor.
Bacterial Wilt	Sudden wilting of individual vines, followed by death of almost-mature plants.
Blossom Blight	Fungal growth that looks like tiny black-headed pins covers old blossoms and stem ends of fruits.
Cucumber Mosaic Virus (CMV)	Leaves brittle, mottled with yellow and green; fruits misshapen and badly mottled.
Cucumber Scab	Cucumbers develop dark leaf spots and fruits show brown scabs. Occasional in pumpkins, squash, and muskmelon.

CUCUMBER FAMILY *(continued)*

Curly Top Virus (CTV)	Older leaves yellow, new ones very dark green; production very low.
Downy Mildew (DM)	Yellow-brown patches on leaf tops matched by dark fuzzy sections on leaf undersides.
Powdery Mildew (PM)	Leaves sprinkled with flourlike white powder; plants lose vigor and fruits lack flavor.
Root-Knot Nematodes	Plants grow slowly, can't tolerate drought, show knobby galls on roots.

HEALTHY PLANT TIPS

Cucurbits grow fast, produce, and die. Make several small successive sowings rather than one large planting. Cucumbers, all squash, and watermelon are easy to grow almost anywhere; fancy melons often are picky about weather.

EGGPLANT   *Solanaceae*

DISEASE	SYMPTOMS
Gray Leaf Spot	Irregular, pale, grayish-brown spots appear in older leaves and gradually spread up the plants.
Lesion Nematodes	Plants spindly, can't tolerate drought; root systems stunted; high risk of secondary root-rot diseases.
Phomopsis Blight	Leaf spots with well-defined margins; large rotting spots on fruits marked by concentric circles.
Root-Knot Nematodes	Plants grow slowly, can't tolerate drought, show knobby galls on roots.
Verticillium Wilt	Plants grow slowly. Midday wilting becomes worse until plants wilt to death.

HEALTHY PLANT TIPS

Grow in containers until weather is quite warm, or keep in pots all summer long. Protect from flea beetles in spring.

FIG   *Moraceae*

DISEASE	SYMPTOMS
Crown Gall	Corky globular growths on stems; stunted new growth.
Lesion Nematodes	Plants spindly, can't tolerate drought; root systems stunted; high risk of secondary root-rot diseases.

HEALTHY PLANT TIPS
In cold winter areas, wrap or bury branches to keep them from being winter-killed. Check with your local Extension Service for the best locally adapted varieties.

GRAPE   *Vitaceae*

DISEASE	SYMPTOMS
Anthracnose	Leaf spots with depressed centers become much worse in wet weather. Fruit rots from numerous small sores.
Black Rot	Reddish brown leaf spots, withered blossoms, and fruits that shrink into mummies.
Crown Gall	Corky globular growths on stems or trunk; stunted new growth.
Downy Mildew	Grayish patches on leaf tops mirrored by fuzzy sections on leaf undersides.
Pierce's Disease	Leaves turn brown; plants lose vigor and slowly die within three to five years.
Powdery Mildew	Leaves and/or fruits covered with white powder, especially in late summer.

HEALTHY PLANT TIPS
Rake up fallen fruit and leaves promptly. Prune plants in late winter, and replace old mulch with new material before the weather warms in spring.

LETTUCE Compositae

DISEASE	SYMPTOMS
Aster Yellows	Inner leaves small, crinkled, and sickly yellow-brown; heads remain soft.
Damping-Off	Seedlings fall over and die during their first month of life.
Downy Mildew	Brownish yellow patches on leaf tops mirrored by fuzzy sections on leaf undersides.
Gray Mold (Botrytis)	Crowded young plants shrivel and have gray fungal masses around base.
Lettuce Mosaic Virus	Leaves mottled with yellow and dark green; dark streaks in ribs.
Powdery Mildew	Leaves sprinkled with flourlike white powder; plants lose vigor.
Soft Rot (Lettuce Drop)	Heads become slimy, outer leaves rot, and cottony white mold develops on base of plant.

HEALTHY PLANT TIPS
Grows best in spring and fall when the weather is cool. Provide shade when lettuce is grown in midsummer. Grow quickly; provide copious water as plants near maturity. Make several small plantings instead of a single large one.

OKRA Malvaceae

DISEASE	SYMPTOMS
Blossom Blight	Fuzzy growth that resembles a thousand tiny black-headed pins covers old blossoms.
Damping-Off	Young seedlings wilt and die; roots rot and stems may blacken close to soil line.
Root-Knot Nematodes	Plants grow slowly, can't tolerate drought, show knobby galls on roots. Highly susceptible.

WHAT'S AILING MY GARDEN? **169**

OKRA (continued)

HEALTHY PLANT TIPS

Needs warm weather and resents root-knot nematodes, but otherwise is very easy to grow. Harvest pods when they are less than five inches long or they may be tough.

ONION FAMILY   *Liliaceae*

onions, garlic, leeks, chives, shallot

DISEASE	SYMPTOMS
Downy Mildew	Grayish purple fuzzy patches on older leaves, or gray to black fuzzy mildew on stored onions.
Fusarium Wilt	Bulbs soft, show brown between rings, and rot in storage.
Pink Root	Sickly, dwarfed plants have few roots; existing roots appear pink.
Purple Blotch (Alternaria Blight)	Watersoaked spots on leaves quickly turn brown and become larger; disease spreads fast.
Rust	Leaves turn yellow and fall over.
Soft Rot	White cottony rot appears on plant base or bulbs; plants become slimy and roots rot.
Stem Nematodes	Seedlings develop bumps on stems and grow very slowly or die; bulbs spongy and rotten.

HEALTHY PLANT TIPS

Rotate plantings of all onions, including perennial types, to avoid insects and diseases. Avoid subjecting bulbing onions to cold or drought. Grow bulb onions adapted to your climate — short-day varieties in the South, and long-day varieties in the North.

PEA (SEE ALSO SOUTHERN PEA) — *Leguminosae*

DISEASE	SYMPTOMS
Downy Mildew (DM)	Leaves become watersoaked, flimsy, and may show white mold.
Fusarium Wilt	Stunted plants turn pale yellow-green, often die shortly after blossoming.
Pea Enation Virus (PEV)	On leaf undersides, yellowish spots turn white and crack open; new growth twisted and dwarfed.
Pea Mosaic Virus	Leaves mottled with yellow, crinkled, with light veins; new growth stunted and lopsided.
Powdery Mildew (PM)	Leaves sprinkled with flourlike white powder; plants lose vigor.
Stem Nematodes	Seedlings develop bumps on stems and grow very slowly or die.

HEALTHY PLANT TIPS
Grow in cool weather, spring and fall. Inoculate seeds before planting. Trellis vines to keep them off the ground.

PEACH — *Rosaceae*

DISEASE	SYMPTOMS
Brown Rot	Fruits become covered with brown mold as they ripen; shrunken mummified fruits hang on trees.
Crown Gall	Corky globular growths on stems; stunted new growth.
Lesion Nematodes	Plants spindly, can't tolerate drought; root systems stunted; high risk of secondary root-rot diseases.

Peach Leaf Curl	New leaves puckered and curled, may drop early; disfigured green fruits.
Peach Mosaic Virus	New stems dwarfed; leaves mottled with yellow; fruits small and misshapen.
Peach Phony Virus	New growth dwarfed, dark green, and lateral rather than upright; overall tree health declines.
Peach X Virus	Leaves speckled with yellow and red, curl upward; mature green fruits drop off.
Powdery Mildew	Leaves and/or fruits covered with white powder, especially in late summer.
Root-Knot Nematodes	Plants grow slowly, can't tolerate drought, show knobby galls on roots.

HEALTHY PLANT TIPS

Choose locally adapted varieties, and prune every winter. Rake up all fallen fruits and leaves. Spray with dormant oil in early winter, fungicide (if indicated) just before buds swell in late winter.

PEAR   *Rosaceae*

DISEASE	SYMPTOMS
Fire Blight	Young twigs and attached leaves blacken and die; shrunken cankers appear on larger stems.
Scab	Corky patches on fruit, often at the stem end.

HEALTHY PLANT TIPS

Choose locally adapted varieties. Trim damaged limbs promptly, and prune to shape trees in winter. Gather fruits when they are still hard but have reached full size; allow to ripen indoors.

PEANUT
Leguminosae

DISEASE	SYMPTOMS
Cercospora Leaf Spot	Circular, slightly raised leaf spots with defined margins; some leaves drop off.
Root-Knot Nematodes	Plants grow slowly, can't tolerate drought, show knobby galls on roots.

HEALTHY PLANT TIPS
Grow in warm, well-drained soil. Weed and cultivate early, but stop cultivating when flower pegs have dropped to the ground.

PEPPER (SWEET AND HOT)
Solanaceae

DISEASE	SYMPTOMS
Blossom Blight	Fuzzy growth that looks like numerous tiny black-headed pins covers blossom ends of fruit.
Cucumber Mosaic Virus (CMV)	Older leaves mottled with brown and may fall off; fruits show small yellowish circles.
Gray Leaf Spot	Irregular pale grayish brown spots appear in older leaves and gradually spread up the plants.
Lesion Nematodes	Plants spindly, can't tolerate drought; root systems stunted; high risk of secondary root rot diseases.
Potato Virus Y (PVY)	Leaves show very light mottling and may drop off; production is poor.
Powdery Mildew	Leaves sprinkled with flourlike white powder; plants lose vigor.
Root-Knot Nematodes (N)	Plants grow slowly, can't tolerate drought, show knobby galls on roots.
Southern Bacterial Wilt	Plants begin to wilt on hot days. Wilting becomes worse and individual or closely spaced plants die.

Southern Blight

In midsummer, plants wilt to death and a white ring develops around the main stem at the soil line.

Tobacco Etch Virus (TEV)

Leaves show brown spots and scratches, with crinkles; fruits small and misshapen.

Tobacco Mosaic Virus (TMV)

Yellowish mottled leaves with light leaf veins, new leaves crinkled and small; misshapen fruit.

HEALTHY PLANT TIPS

Set out plants in warm soil, but expect modest production until fall. Water as needed to relieve heat and water stress. Ripe peppers are much sweeter than green ones.

PLUM   *Rosaceae*

DISEASE	SYMPTOMS
Brown Rot	Fruits become covered with brown mold as they ripen; shrunken mummified fruits hang on trees.
Crown Gall	Corky globular growths on stems; stunted new growth.
Peach Mosaic Virus	New stems dwarfed, leaves mottled with yellow; fruits small and misshapen.

HEALTHY PLANT TIPS

Plums mature faster than peaches, so there is less time for trouble to develop. Prune trees aggressively in winter. In summer and fall, gather up all fallen fruits and leaves.

POTATO   *Solanaceae*

DISEASE	SYMPTOMS
Alternaria (Early Blight)	Very small circular leaf spots on older leaves become numerous, run together; leaves shrivel and die, remain attached to plant.

Anthracnose	Dark sunken sores on stems at the soil line.
Cyst Nematodes	Plants grow slowly, can't tolerate drought, show stunted roots, and don't produce well.
Late Blight	Brown blotches on leaves, gray underneath, often spreading from leaf centers.
Potato Virus Y	Leaves show light streaks or mottling, some drop off.
Powdery Mildew	Leaves sprinkled with flourlike white powder; plants lose vigor.
Root-Knot Nematodes	Plants grow slowly, can't tolerate drought, show knobby galls on roots.
Scurf	Scabby blisters on skin which become silver-gray in color.
Southern Bacterial Wilt	Plants begin to wilt on hot days. Wilting becomes worse and individual or closely spaced plants die.

HEALTHY PLANT TIPS

Where disease pressure is severe, grow early varieties. Protect tubers from sunlight as they grow and during harvest. Mulch reduces insect problems and may increase root size.

RADISH   *Cruciferae*

HEALTHY PLANT TIPS

Radishes grow so quickly that they rarely host diseases, especially in home gardens where they are rotated often. Flea beetles sometimes make small holes in plants' leaves. The best radishes grow quickly in spring and fall, when soil temperatures are moderate. Provide water to encourage fast, uninterrupted growth.

RASPBERRY

DISEASE	SYMPTOMS
Anthracnose	Leaf spots with depressed centers become much worse in wet weather. Fruits rot from numerous small sores.
Crown Gall	Corky globular growths on canes; stunted new growth.
Double Blossom Rosette	Blooms lopsided and misshapen with leaflets inside, often in clusters; reduced fruit set.
Powdery Mildew	Leaves appear to have white powder sprinkled on them; vigor declines.
Raspberry Mosaic Virus	Slow growth, mottled leaves with curled down edges; poor fruit quality and low production.
Rust	Powdery orange deposits on leaf undersides; leaves die and drop off.

HEALTHY PLANT TIPS
Prepare planting holes in advance. Use disease-free, locally adapted varieties. Mulch with straw and compost to reduce weeds and maintain soil moisture.

ROSE

DISEASE	SYMPTOMS
Anthracnose	Leaf spots with depressed centers become much worse in wet weather. Rose hips rot from numerous small sores.
Black Spot	Dark circles with fringed edges on upper sides of leaves.
Crown Gall	Corky globular growths on canes, often near soil line; stunted new growth.
Fusarium Wilt	Plants grow slowly, wilt on hot days, older leaves turn yellow. Small fibrous roots rot.

ROSE (continued)

Powdery Mildew

Leaves sprinkled with flourlike white powder; plants lose vigor.

Root-Knot Nematodes

Plants grow slowly, can't tolerate drought, show knobby galls on roots.

Rust

Powdery orange deposits on leaf undersides. Leaves die and drop off.

Southern Blight

In midsummer, plants wilt to death and a white ring develops around the main stem at the soil line.

HEALTHY PLANT TIPS

Experiment with different types to find roses you like that stand up well in your climate. Sacrifice those that grow poorly.

SOUTHERN PEA   *Leguminosae*

crowders, blackeyes, purple hull, lady peas

DISEASE	SYMPTOMS
Cercospora Leaf Spot	Circular spots on old leaves have yellowish margins; some leaves drop off.

HEALTHY PLANT TIPS

Plant after the soil is quite warm. Southern peas are very easy to grow in warm climates. They also may be used as a summer cover crop.

SPINACH   *Chenopodiaceae*

DISEASE	SYMPTOMS
Anthracnose	Watery blotches, often on leaf edges, appear suddenly and spread in rainy weather.
Cucumber Mosaic Virus (CMV)	New leaves yellow and small, older leaves mottled and crinkled; plants decline steadily.
Downy Mildew (DM)	Purplish patches on leaf tops mirrored by fuzzy sections on leaf undersides.

White Rust

Light blisters on leaf undersides
that erupt and exude chalky white
powder.

HEALTHY PLANT TIPS
Grow quickly in spring and fall, when the weather is cool. Spinach is winter
hardy in many areas; new leaves from overwintered plants are very sweet.
All spinach bolts in late spring, when days become long and warm.

STRAWBERRY   *Rosaceae*

DISEASE

SYMPTOMS

Gray Mold (Botrytis)

Cottony gray mold forms on fruit
close to ground or stored in refrigerator.

Lesion Nematodes

Plants spindly, can't tolerate
drought; root systems stunted; high
risk of secondary root-rot diseases.

Powdery Mildew

Leaves sprinkled with flourlike
white powder; plants lose vigor.
Usually appears in late summer.

Red Stele

Plants decline as roots rot; interior
of roots shows red coloring.

Root-Knot Nematodes

Plants grow slowly, can't tolerate
drought, show knobby galls on roots.

Stem Nematodes

Plants develop bumps on young
stems and grow very slowly or die.

Strawberry Stunt Virus

New growth small; leaves papery
and curled; blossom stems weak;
little fruit produced.

Strawberry Viruses

Stunted plants; mosaic or yellow
mottling on leaves; decline in overall plant health.

HEALTHY PLANT TIPS
Enrich soil with compost and other organic matter before planting. For top
quality, start new beds with new plants every four years. Weed and clean
beds in fall and mulch with fresh material.

SWEETPOTATO   *Convolvulaceae*

DISEASE	SYMPTOMS
Black Rot	Potatoes have corky-textured black spots, sometimes large; black fuzz sometimes visible.
Fusarium Wilt	Plants grow slowly, wilt on hot days, stems rot and older leaves turn yellow and wither.
Root-Knot Nematodes	Plants grow slowly, can't tolerate drought, show knobby galls on roots.
Scurf	Dark brown to black spots on skin, sometimes covering most of the tuber.
White Rust	Yellowish blisters on leaf undersides erupt and exude chalky white powder.

HEALTHY PLANT TIPS
Rotate crop location every three years. Choose warm, well-drained spots. Easy to grow where warm weather lasts into fall.

TOMATO   *Solanaceae*

DISEASE	SYMPTOMS
Alternaria (Early Blight)	Small brown spots on lower leaves expand, develop concentric circles, and become numerous until leaves shrivel and die, remaining attached to plant.
Buckeye Rot	Fruits that touch the ground develop brown spots with concentric brown circles around them.
Cucumber Mosaic Virus (CMV)	Leaves narrow and stringy, new growth stunted; fruits mottled with light yellow-green.
Curly Top Virus	New growth twisted and stiff, with much yellowing of leaves.
Damping-Off	Seedlings fall over and die during their first month of life.
Fusarium Wilt (F, FF)	Leaves turn yellow and wilt. Conditions become worse gradually; plants usually die before fruit is fully ripe.

Gray Leaf Spot	Irregular pale grayish brown spots appear in older leaves and gradually spread up the plants.
Late Blight	Brown leaf blotches, gray underneath, often starting at leaf centers on older leaves. Fruit spots grayish green.
Lesion Nematodes	Plants spindly, can't tolerate drought; root systems stunted; high risk of secondary root-rot diseases.
Root-Knot Nematode (N)	Plants grow slowly, can't tolerate drought, show knobby galls on roots.
Septoria Leaf Spot	Small spots with dark brown margins and lighter centers sprinkled on leaf tops; leaves turn yellow.
Soft Rot	Cottony dry mold on lower stems, hard black mouse droppings inside stems or in ruptures on stems.
Southern Bacterial Wilt	Plants begin to wilt on hot days. Wilting becomes worse and individual or closely spaced plants die.
Southern Blight	In midsummer, plants wilt to death and a white ring develops around the main stem at the soil line.
Spotted Wilt Virus	New leaves show numerous small dots and wilt rapidly; green fruits misshapen with faint concentric circles.
Tobacco Mosaic Virus (T)	Leaves mottled with dark green and light yellow-green; plants stunted; fruit mottled and scarred.
Verticillium Wilt (V)	Plants grow slowly when infected early. After fruit set, midday wilting becomes worse until plants wilt to death.

HEALTHY PLANT TIPS

Provide plenty of water early in the season, then slack off. Mulch heavily, and stake, cage, or trellis plants. Although the above list is long, tomatoes are really not difficult to grow, especially when resistant varieties are used.

INDEX

Page numbers in *italics* indicate illustrations.

A

Agrobacterium tumefaciens. See Crown gall

Airborne diseases, 11, 53–54; detailed descriptions of, 54–85, 63, 72, 75, 80

Albugo candida. See White rust

Albugo occidentalis. See White rust

Alfalfa meal, 152

Almond, 68, 101

Alternaria blight, 89–92, 163, 170, 174, 179

Alternaria dauci. See Alternaria blight; Early blight

Alternaria solani. See Alternaria blight; Damping-off; Early blight

Alternaria stem canker, 92

Alyssum, 49, 67

Amaranth, 49

Ammonium sulfate, 50

Angular leaf spot, 92, 166

Anthracnose, 53, 160, 161, 166, 168, 175–77; detailed description of, 54–57

Aphids, 5, 9, 86, 111, 113, 117–18, 121, 124–26; bean, 115–16, 123, 129; cabbage, 115–16; cotton, 115–16; lily, 116; pea, 122–23; peach, 115–16, 120, 122–23, 129; potato, 116, 122; southern pea, 115; strawberry, 128–29; turnip, 115

Apple, 57–59, 74–76, 79, 139; symptom guide, 159

Apple scab, 57–59, 159

Apricot, 68, 124, 159

Arugula, 109, 145

Asparagus, 34, 36, 38–40, 61; symptom guide, 160

Asparagus rust, 61

Aster, 27, 34, 114–15, *114*, 164, 169

Aster yellows, 114–15, *114*, 164, 169

B

Bacteria, 6, 10, 13, 19–21, 133, 140; detailed description of, 7–9. *See also specific diseases;* Insect-vectored bacterial diseases

Bacterial blight. *See* Black rot of cabbage

Bacterial wilt of corn, 108–9, 166

Bacterial wilt of cucumber, 105–7, *105*, 166

Baking soda, 40, 82, 99

Bark, shredded, 30, 149

Basil, 49

Bean, 10, 11, 13–15, 34, 36, 39, 44, 46–47, 54–56, 59–62, 64, 77–79, 81, 86, 95, 110, 118–19, 123, 135, 139, 140, 142, 148–49; bush, 14–15, 59, 62, 148; dry, 59, 115–16; fava, 123; lima, 59, 116; pinto, 13; pole, 59, 62; scarlet runner, 59; snap, 59, 78, 115–16; soy-, 13, 95; symptom guides, 145–47, 160–61

Bean mosaic virus, 115–16, 160

Bean rust, 59–62

Bees, 106

Beet, 83, 95–96, 109, 152–53; sugar, 118–19, 138; symptom guide, 161

Beetles, 5, 144; cucumber, 105–7; flea, 108–9, 145, 167, 175; Japanese, 10, 146; lady, 113, 116, 125; nocturnal, 146; symptoms of damage, 145–46

Bermuda grass, 155

Lime, 44, 148–49, 152–53; -sulfur, 40, 57, 61, 88, 102

Loganberry, 41–42

Longidorus. See Nematodes, needle

M

Magnesium, 152–53

Maize chlorotic dwarf virus, 122, 165; detailed description of, 120–21

Maize dwarf mosaic virus, 121–22, 165

Manganese, 153

Manure, 14, 17, 38–40, 50, 160; airborne diseases and, 70, 77; nematodes and, 136–37; nutritional disorders and, 150, 152–53; soilborne diseases and, 26–27, 39–40, 50

Maple, 155

Marigold, dwarf, 136

Meloidognye. See Nematodes, root-knot

Melon, 30, 34, 36, 47, 73–74, 105–7, 116, 118; musk-, 29, 49, 55, 79, 81, 92, 105, 107, 135, 166–67; symptom guides, 147, 166–67. *See also* Watermelon

Milk mixture, 131

Milkweed, 118

Mint, 49

Mites, 86, 113, 107, 124, 147

Monarda, 49, 79

Monilina fructicola. See Brown rot
Monilina laxa. See Brown rot
Monilina urnula. See Mummy berry

Monilochaetes infuscans. See Scurf

Morning glory, 66–67

Mosaic, defined, 112

Mottle, defined, 112

Mulch, 15, 35, 48, 69, 160, 162, 175, 178, 180; airborne diseases and, 57; insect-vectored virus diseases and, 128; nematodes and, 137, 143; nutritional disorders and, 150; soilborne diseases and, 21–22, 39–40

Mummy berry, 68–70, 162

Mustard, 13, 49, 62; symptom guides, 145, 162–63

Mycoplasmas, 9

N

Nasturtium, 49, 118

Nectarine, 68, 70, 101, 124

Nematodes, 5, 11, 17, 36, 52, 132–34, *134*; beneficial, 10; bulb, 142–43; compost and, 136–37, 143; cover cropping and, 141; cyst, 138–39, 161, 163, 175; dagger, 141–42; detailed descriptions of, 9–10, 135–43, *136, 140*; lesion, 139–41, *140*, 159, 164, 165, 167, 168, 171, 173, 178, 180; manure and, 136–37; mulch and, 137, 143; needle, 141–42; root-knot, 135–39, *136*, 160, 164, 167, 169–70, 172, 173, 175, 177–80; rotation of crops and, 134, 136, 139, 142–43; stem, 142–43, 161, 166, 170, 171, 178; sting, 141–42; stunt, 141–42

Nitrogen, 149, 152

Northern corn leaf blight, 100–101, *101*, 165

Nutritional disorders, disease-like, 148–54, *151*

O

Okra, 24, 135–36; symptom guides, 145–47, 169–70

Onion, 40–41, 44, 61, 71, *72*, 73, 89–91, 137, 142; symptom guides, 146–47, 170

Onion rust, 61

Oxalis, 49

P

Pansy, 49

Parsley, 50, 114, 139

Pea, 39, 54, 61, 64, 79, 81, 139, 142, 149, 154; Alderman, 123; southern, 13–15, 24, 34, 47, 95–96, 116, 122, 145, 147, 177; symptom guides, 145, 147, 171, 177

R

Radish, 62, 107, 109, 145, 175

Ragweed, 118

Raspberry, 10, 27, 40, 57, 70–71, 125–27, 153; Cuthbert, 126; Fallgold, 126; symptom guide, 176

Raspberry mosaic virus, 125–27, 162, 176

Raspberry yellow virus, 125–27

Red stele, 41–42, 178

Rhizobia, 149

Rhizoctonia solani. See Damping-off

Rickettsia. See Pierce's disease

Rock phosphate, 152

Root maggots, 10, 146

Rose, 27–28, 54, 56–57, 61, 74, 93, 93; antique, 92; hybrid tea, 92, 94; symptom guides, 146, 176–77; yellow, 92, 95

Rose rust, 61

Rotation of crops, 16–17, 52, 146, 170, 179; airborne diseases and, 61–64, 67, 73, 78, 85; importance of, 11–12; leaf-spot diseases and, 91–92, 96, 103; nematodes and, 134, 136, 139, 142–43; soilborne diseases and, 21–22, 25, 27, 30, 42–44, 47–48, 50, 52

Rust, 161, 162, 165, 170, 176, 177. *See also* White rust

Rutabaga, 62

Rye, 13

S

Sabadilla dust, 109, 146, 147

Sage, 49

Salt, 155

Salvia, 79

Scale, 146

Scallion, 40, 41

Sclerotinia. See Lettuce drop; Soft rot; Stem rot; Watery rot

Sclerotium rolfsii. See Southern blight

Scurf, 43–44, 175, 179

Seaweed/kelp, 150, 151, 153

Septoria apii. See Celery late blight

Septoria leaf spot, 97, 98, 164, 180; detailed description of, 102–3

Septoria lycopersici. See Septoria leaf spot

Shallot, 170

Shield bugs, 147

Snapdragon, 49, 54

Soft rot, 44–46, 45, 160, 163, 164, 169, 170, 180

Soilborne diseases, 12, 19–23, 129; detailed descriptions of, 24–52, 28, 31, 37, 45

Solarization of soil, 22, 46, 137, 142–43; detailed description of, 23

Sorghum, 13

Sorghum halepense. See Johnson grass

Southern bacterial wilt, 46–47, 173, 175, 180

Southern blight, 47–48, 174, 177, 180

Southern corn leaf blight, 100–101, 101, 166

Spinach, 34, 54, 71, 73–74, 83–84, 110, 114, 116–18, 130, 140, 150; New Zealand, 114; symptom guides, 145, 177–78

Spinach blight, 116–18

Spondylocladium atrovirens. See Scurf

Spotted wilt virus, 127–28, 180

Squash, 13, 24–25, 29–30, 44, 79, 92, 105, 116, 118–19, 151–53; summer, 24–25, 92, 166–67; symptom guides, 147, 166–67; winter, 92, 166–67

Squash bugs, 147

Stemphylium solani. See Gray leaf spot

Stem rot, 44–46, 45

Sterilization of soil, 22–23, 32, 46, 52, 64

Stewart's wilt, 108–9, 166

Stink bugs, 147

Stock, 49, 67

Strawberry, 7, 36–42, 49, 51, 79, 128–29, 135–36, 139, 142, 153; symptom guides, 147, 178